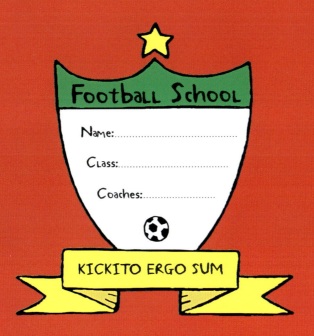

Football School

Name:......................................

Class:......................................

Coaches:...................................

KICKITO ERGO SUM

First published 2023 by Walker Books Ltd
87 Vauxhall Walk, London SE11 5HJ

2 4 6 8 10 9 7 5 3 1

British Library Cataloguing in Publication Data:
a catalogue record for this book is available from the British Library

ISBN 978-1-5295-0758-4

www.walker.co.uk
footballschool.co

WALKER BOOKS
AND SUBSIDIARIES
LONDON • BOSTON • SYDNEY • AUCKLAND

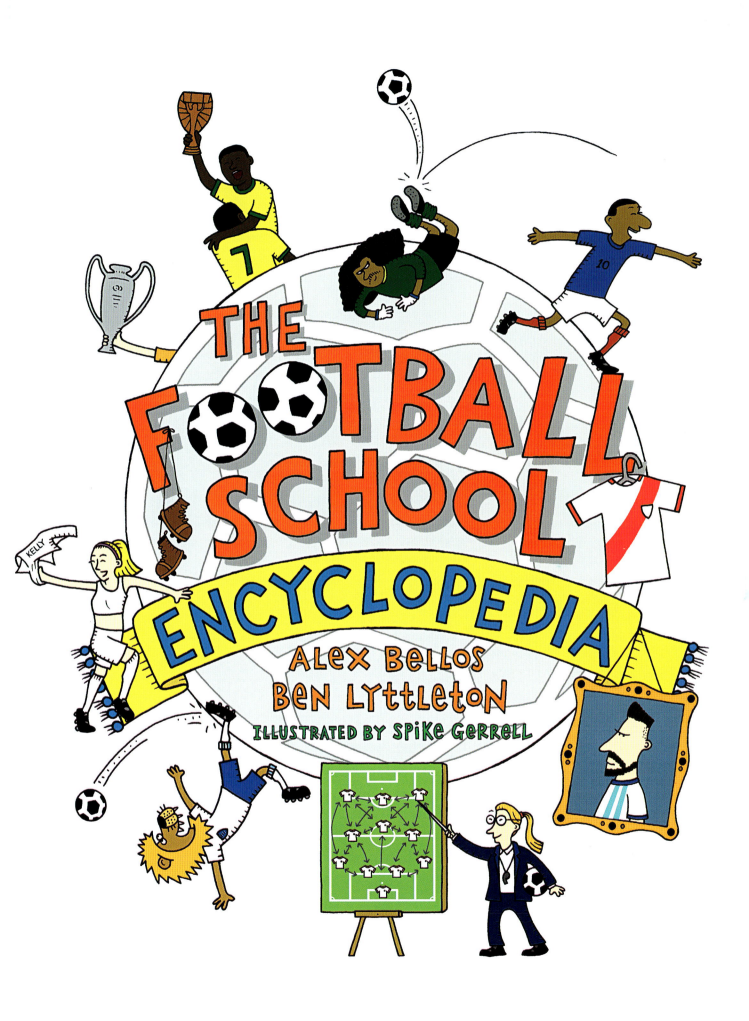

THE FOOTBALL SCHOOL

ENCYCLOPEDIA

Alex Bellos
Ben Lyttleton

ILLUSTRATED BY Spike Gerrell

-CONTENTS-

Here's what is in the book — enjoy the contents!

I certainly will — I'm always content!

-INTRODUCTION-

Welcome to *The Football School Encyclopedia!* It's a book of facts and so let's start with an important one: football is the best sport in the world. OK, you knew that one already. But we have lots more lined up for you. In FACT, we promise you will discover something new and surprising about football on every page. Fact!

At Football School we love the game and we are always looking to tell amazing, true stories about it. In this book, we have cast our net widely. We have strength in depth! Yes, you will learn about famous players and the world's top clubs, but you will also explore history and science and business and language and much, much more. We want to celebrate everyone and everything in football. All together now!

We kick off with an overview of this curious sport involving two teams of eleven players in which the object is to kick a leather sphere through a large rectangle. In the first section, THE GAME, we journey through football's past from ancient history to the present day. We'll explain what the rules are, how the game is played, what equipment is needed and we'll end with a roll-call of its greatest heroes. Respect!

Next, we travel the globe. The second section, THE CLUBS, contains football maps of the UK, Europe and the world. You'll never get lost going to a match again! You'll read about stadiums and league pyramids and transfer windows. Want to find out what it is like to dress up in a pie costume? We've mascot it covered!

Now to raise the flag on the third section, THE COUNTRIES, where you will admire the 211 flags and shirt colours of every national football team recognized by FIFA, the sport's governing body. We'll also take you on a safari of their nicknames, from The Antelopes to The Zebras. Hoof it up, mate! Every player dreams of winning the World Cup and we'll show you a highlight reel of every final from 1930 to 2022. Yes, reel-y!

If you have ever wondered what footballers do all day, all is revealed in section four, THE FOOTBALL FAMILY, in which we examine the daily lives of people who work in the game. We'll give you an appetizing pre-match menu and details of how to recuperate afterwards. You'll also learn about coaches, referees, scouts, data analysts and many other roles in football you may never have heard about. We also meet the sport's most fanatical fans. Fan-cy that!

The ref is looking at their watch. It's almost the end of the book. But not before section five, FOOTBALL EVERYWHERE, which celebrates many different ways we enjoy football, from reading about it, to talking about it, to arguing about it, to playing it on mud, on sand and on the computer. Oh, what a joy(stick)! And as the referee blows the final whistle, we explore what football may look like many years from now. It's the foot-ure!

At the end of each section, there's a brain-busting quiz. You'll be tested on some of the amazing facts in this book. And here's our final fact for this page: by the end of the book, you will be bursting with football knowledge! Now let's get on with it! Enjoy!

Alex and Ben

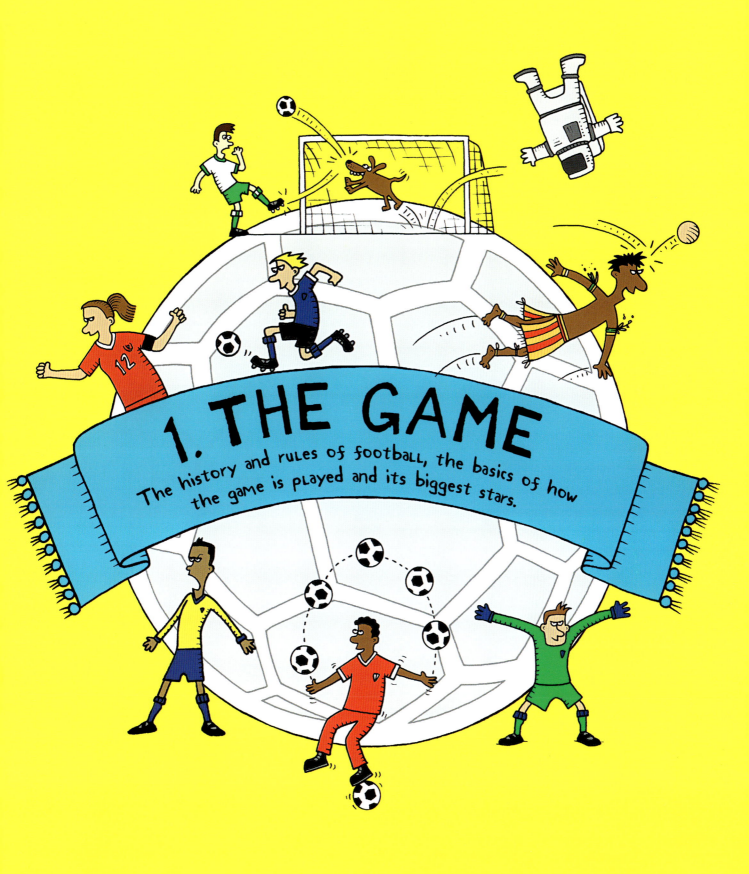

1. THE GAME

The history and rules of football, the basics of how the game is played and its biggest stars.

-THE ANCIENT ORIGINS-
OF FOOTBALL

For thousands of years people all over the world have loved playing ball games. These ancient sports all came before the football we know today.

AFRICA
EGYPT

The ancient Egyptians played a team ball game, similar to hockey, using palm branches as sticks and a ball made from papyrus wrapped in animal skin. Paintings from around 1000 BC and earlier show they also took part in other sports like rhythmic gymnastics, archery, tug-of-war, juggling and handball too. Pharaoh-nuff!

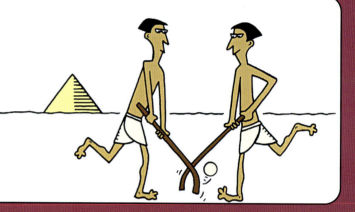

EUROPE
GREECE

The ancient Greeks liked playing ball games – usually with no clothes on. A famous engraving from around 400 BC shows a naked man balancing a ball on his thigh, looking just like he is playing keepy-uppy. Cheeky!

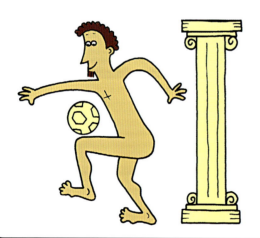

EUROPE
ROME

The ancient Romans played many ball games. Some games used a small, hard ball filled with feathers and others used a bladder filled with air. The Romans also built impressive stadiums, such as the Colosseum in around 70 AD, to watch fights and chariot races. Legion!

SOUTH AMERICA
BRAZIL

Indigenous communities in the Amazon Rainforest have long made balls from the latex of rubber trees. In 1900, the first European explorer to encounter the Pareci people of Brazil found them playing a game in which two teams bounced a rubber ball back and forth with their heads. Brazilliant!

NORTH AMERICA
MEXICO

The civilizations that lived in Mexico between 1500 BC and 1500 AD – including the Olmec, Aztec and Maya – all played team ball games. The matches were important religious rituals and some historians believe the losers' heads were chopped off and the skulls used as balls. My-o-Maya!

ASIA
CHINA

Played from around 200 BC to around 1400 AD, the Chinese team game *cuju* had many versions, including one with a net suspended between two poles in the middle of the pitch. The aim was to kick the ball through a small opening in the net. Goal-in-the-hole!

ASIA
JAPAN

The Japanese game *kemari* was played from around 600 AD to around 1900. Players dressed in formal robes and would kick the ball in the air as many times as possible without it touching the ground. One team are said to have kept the ball up for 1,000 kicks. Grand!

OCEANIA
AUSTRALIA

Marn grook is a team game that uses a ball made from possum skin and is played by the Indigenous peoples of Australia. It was first written about in the nineteenth century by the Europeans who settled there. Players would hold the ball in their hands, let it fall and then kick it high. *Marn*-ifique!

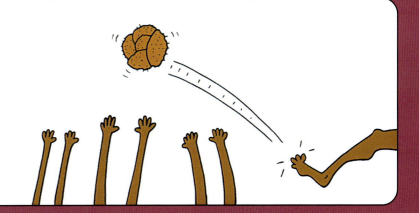

London mayor bans football

The mayor's decree is the earliest written mention of football. At this time it is a kind of mass brawl in which a mob of players chase a ball, with almost no rules. No wonder it annoys the authorities!

1314

Edward IV bans football

In the fifteenth century, mob football remains popular, despite many more attempts to outlaw it. King Edward IV passes a law saying that instead of playing football, people should be practising archery. Target man!

1477

-A SHORT-
HISTORY OF FOOTBALL

In the late Middle Ages, football was the name of an unregulated and violent British game. Here are some important dates in the story of how this game evolved to become the most popular sport in the world.

1747

1660

Posh boys play ball

Football is popular at upper-class schools like Eton, Harrow and Westminster. Poet Thomas Gray writes a poem about football at Eton. He writes that the "rolling circle" gives "fearful joy". Poetry in motion!

Game gets gate

Scientist Francis Willughby, an expert on birds, insects and sports, writes the earliest account of football involving a pitch and a goal. The pitch is "a close that has a gate at either end. The gates are called goals."

1762

1848

Mob football still thrills

Among the lower classes, mob football remains widespread. The annual Shrove Tuesday game at Alnwick, Northumberland – in which two competing hordes aim to get a ball from one side of the town to another – is a hit. This game still takes place today!

Students write rules

A group of Cambridge University students write the first-ever set of "official" rules for football, to draw a line between it and rugby, the game played at Rugby School.

Scribe writes match report

The earliest description of kicking and dribbling appears in a Latin manuscript from around this time. It says that young men "propel a huge ball not by throwing it into the air but by striking it and rolling it along the ground … with their feet".

1481

King orders boots

King Henry VIII asks his personal shoemaker, Cornelius Johnson, to make him a pair of boots for playing football. They haven't survived but historians think they were ankle-high and made from leather.

1526

Come on lads, let's keep it old school!

Am I so round with you as you with me, That like a football you do spurn me thus?

1594

"Football," quoth the Bard

The game is popular enough for William Shakespeare to mention it in his play *The Comedy of Errors*. Not goalkeeping errors, of course!

1581

Football enters schools

A report by a London headmaster describes football as a game for students between two small sides that is good for health and strength, an early indication that a less violent version of the game would flourish in schools.

1857

First football club is born

Two members of a cricket club in Sheffield start a club just for football, Sheffield FC, the world's first football club. A wealthy city thanks to its steel factories, Sheffield becomes an early hub of the game.

1863

FA introduces Laws of the Game

A group of clubs and schools found the Football Association to decide on common rules, set out in the Laws of the Game. With a national body, the stage is set for football to grow and grow.

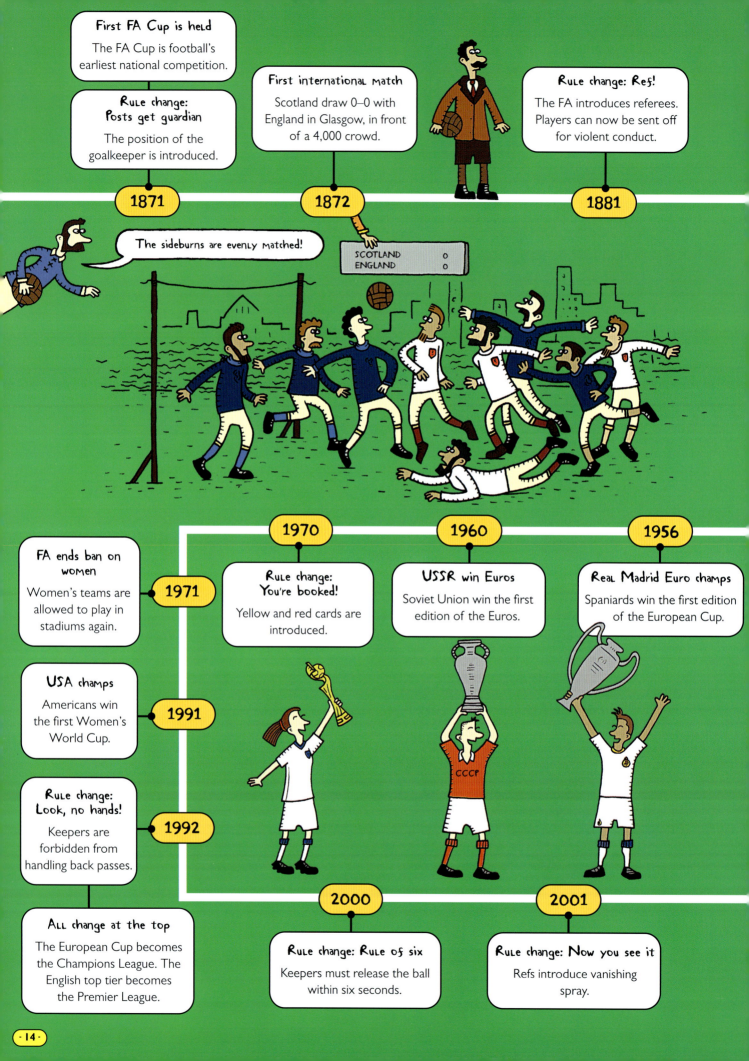

First FA Cup is held
The FA Cup is football's earliest national competition.

Rule change: Posts get guardian
The position of the goalkeeper is introduced.

First international match
Scotland draw 0–0 with England in Glasgow, in front of a 4,000 crowd.

Rule change: Ref!
The FA introduces referees. Players can now be sent off for violent conduct.

1871

1872

1881

The sideburns are evenly matched!

SCOTLAND 0
ENGLAND 0

1970

1960

1956

FA ends ban on women
Women's teams are allowed to play in stadiums again.

1971

Rule change: You're booked!
Yellow and red cards are introduced.

USSR win Euros
Soviet Union win the first edition of the Euros.

Real Madrid Euro champs
Spaniards win the first edition of the European Cup.

USA champs
Americans win the first Women's World Cup.

1991

Rule change: Look, no hands!
Keepers are forbidden from handling back passes.

1992

CCCP

All change at the top
The European Cup becomes the Champions League. The English top tier becomes the Premier League.

2000

2001

Rule change: Rule of six
Keepers must release the ball within six seconds.

Rule change: Now you see it
Refs introduce vanishing spray.

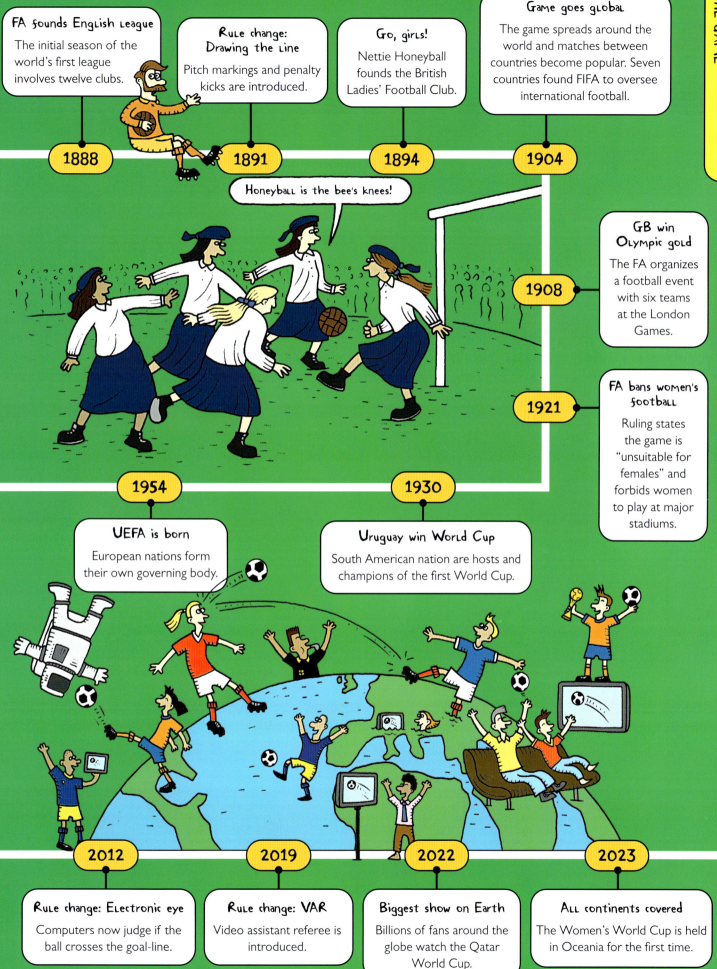

FA founds English league

The initial season of the world's first league involves twelve clubs.

1888

Rule change: Drawing the line

Pitch markings and penalty kicks are introduced.

1891

Go, girls!

Nettie Honeyball founds the British Ladies' Football Club.

1894

Game goes global

The game spreads around the world and matches between countries become popular. Seven countries found FIFA to oversee international football.

1904

Honeyball is the bee's knees!

GB win Olympic gold

The FA organizes a football event with six teams at the London Games.

1908

FA bans women's football

Ruling states the game is "unsuitable for females" and forbids women to play at major stadiums.

1921

UEFA is born

European nations form their own governing body.

1954

Uruguay win World Cup

South American nation are hosts and champions of the first World Cup.

1930

Rule change: Electronic eye

Computers now judge if the ball crosses the goal-line.

2012

Rule change: VAR

Video assistant referee is introduced.

2019

Biggest show on Earth

Billions of fans around the globe watch the Qatar World Cup.

2022

All continents covered

The Women's World Cup is held in Oceania for the first time.

2023

-THE LAWS OF THE GAME-

Football's rules are written in The Laws of the Game and apply to all professional matches. There are 17 major laws running over 228 pages. If you thought football was simple, think again!

THE MAIN RULES

The Laws state that every professional match starts with a maximum of eleven players on each team, lasts two periods of 45 minutes and the winner is the team that scores the most goals. The Laws are set by an independent organization called the International Football Association Board (IFAB). The referee enforces the Laws, so needs to understand every single one of them.

THE PITCH

The law relating to the Field of Play states that the pitch must be rectangular and each part of the pitch must measure a certain distance. For international matches, the dimensions of the pitch can be different to league matches. The Laws explain that certain actions happen in certain areas of the pitch.

The **goal area** is where goal kicks (a kick taken by the defending team after the attacking team kicks the ball behind the goal-line) are taken from.

The **penalty area** is where goalkeepers can use their hands to catch the ball. Fouls by the defending side here lead to a penalty, taken from the penalty spot.

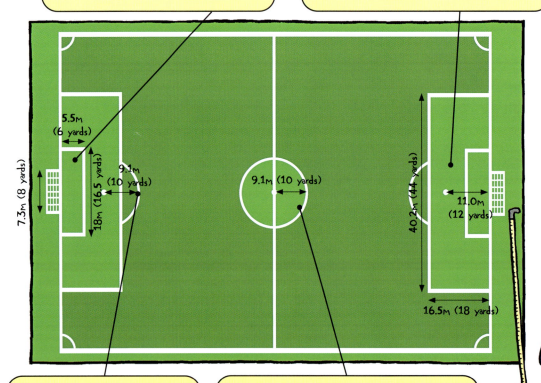

5.5m (6 yards)
7.3m (8 yards)
18m (16.5 yards)
9.1m (10 yards)
9.1m (10 yards)
40.2m (44 yards)
11.0m (12 yards)
16.5m (18 yards)

The **D** on the edge of the penalty area is positioned to make sure that every player, if they are standing outside the D, is at least 10 yards away from the spot, the required distance, when a penalty is taken.

The **centre circle** is used to make sure that at kick-off, when the ball is placed on the centre spot, the opposing team are at least 10 yards away, the required distance. During penalty shoot-outs, all players apart from the goalkeepers and the penalty taker must be in the centre circle.

SCORING GOALS

A goal is scored when the whole ball passes over the goal-line, between the goalposts and under the crossbar, and no foul has been committed. The referee decides if the goal has been scored fairly – but it's not always easy!

GOAL OR NO GOAL?

Which ball below would be awarded as a goal?

The whole of the ball on the left has crossed the line: goal! The ball on the right has not fully crossed the line: no goal!

A player scores but her boot has fallen off before taking the shot.

Goal! If the ball has not gone out of play before the goal, so the player hasn't had a chance to put the boot back on, the goal stands.

A player shoots and the ball hits the referee and then goes into the goal.

No goal! The ref awards possession to the defending team by dropping the ball at the goalkeeper's feet.

A team brought on a sub but forgot to take a player off. That team then concedes.

Goal! The goal would only be disallowed if the team with the extra player had scored and that player had played an active part in the goal.

A dog runs onto the pitch and stops a goal-bound shot from going in.

No goal! The dog is what's called an "outside agent", so the ref gives possession to the defending team's goalkeeper.

The goalkeeper throws the ball directly into the opponents' goal.

No goal! A goal kick is awarded to the defending team, as you cannot score from any kind of throw.

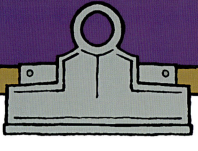

THE OFFSIDE RULE

Some goals are disallowed by the referee because a player is offside. This is one of the most complicated – and controversial – Laws of the Game. Offside ensures that a player must have two opposition players between them and the goal at the moment the ball is passed by a teammate. Specifically, the player is in an offside position if any part of the head, body or feet is nearer to the opponents' goal-line than the ball and the second-last opponent (usually a defender). The rule is in place to stop players hanging around the goal – that would be off!

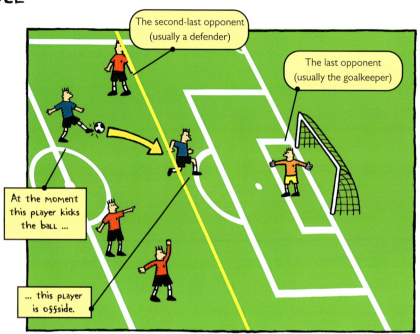

The second-last opponent (usually a defender)

The last opponent (usually the goalkeeper)

At the moment this player kicks the ball ...

... this player is offside.

LAYING DOWN THE LAW

The IFAB meets every year and is always adding new laws to improve the game and cover every eventuality. That means a few laws are obscure and hardly ever come up. Here are some of our favourites – and where they appear in the official Laws of the Game.

Caught you red-handed!

Law 1.1 The Field of Play – Field Surface:

The colour of the pitch must be green even if the pitch is made of artificial material like AstroTurf.

Law 4.3 The Players' Equipment – Colours:

Each team must wear colours that distinguish them from the other team – but if the goalkeepers are wearing the same colour, the match can go ahead.

Law 8.1 The Start and Restart of Play – Kick-Off:

You can score a goal direct from kick-off, but not an own goal. If you pass the ball back to your own goal and it goes in without touching another player, a corner is awarded.

Law 11.3 Offside – No Offence:

You cannot be offside from a goal kick, throw-in or corner.

RED AND YELLOW CARDS

The Laws of the Game exist to keep football fair and to keep players safe. If players misbehave, the referee can punish them by showing a yellow or a red card. Below are some actions that merit a card. Behave!

A **yellow card** is a caution, like a warning. If a player is shown two yellow cards in the same game, they are sent off. A yellow card is shown for these offences:

★ Time-wasting
★ Dissent (disagreeing with the referee)
★ Entering or leaving the field without the referee's permission
★ Failing to respect distance from set-pieces
★ Persistent offences
★ Entering the referee review area (RRA)
★ Excessively using the "review" signal
★ Celebrating in an excessive or provocative way (taking off shirt or wearing a mask)
★ Unsporting behaviour, which includes (but is not limited to) the following:
   ✧ Simulation (faking injury)
   ✧ Reckless fouls
   ✧ Handball to stop an attack or to try and score
   ✧ Showing lack of respect for the game
   ✧ Verbally distracting an opponent

A **red card** is a sending-off, which is when the player has to leave the pitch. It will lead to a ban of at least one game. A red card is shown for these offences:

★ Denying an obvious goal-scoring opportunity [DOGSO] with a foul or handball
★ Serious foul play that endangers the safety of an opponent
★ Biting or spitting at someone
★ Violent conduct
★ Using offensive, insulting or abusive language
★ Entering the video operation room (VOR)
★ Receiving a second caution in the same match

Coaching staff can also be shown a red card. They have to leave their technical area and watch the rest of the match in the stands. This could be for:
★ Showing dissent to match officials
★ Entering the pitch to interfere with play
★ Physical or aggressive behaviour
★ Using insulting language

-IN POSITION-

Football is a team game and each of the positions have different roles. The best teams have players who know exactly what their job is and how to help their teammates around them. Here is a breakdown of the four key positions in the team and their responsibilities on the pitch.

STRIKER

STRIKER

ATTACKING MIDFIELDER

LEFT MIDFIELDER

RIGHT MIDFIELDER

DEFENSIVE MIDFIELDER

CENTRE-BACK

CENTRE-BACK

GOALKEEPER

LEFT-BACK

RIGHT-BACK

ATTACK

The job of the attacker, also known as the striker or forward, is simple: to score goals. These players often take the glory in the big moments, thanks to their ability to find space away from markers, keep cool under pressure and then perfect their shooting into the corners of the goal. Different strikers have different strengths: some, such as **Kylian Mbappé**, are super-fast and others, such as **Cristiano Ronaldo**, are brilliant at heading the ball. The ideal striker would be someone who can combine the speed of **Mbappé**, the positioning of **Robert Lewandowski**, the finishing of **Vivianne Miedema**, the anticipation of **Karim Benzema**, the heading of **Ronaldo**, the composure of **Sam Kerr**, the vision of **Lionel Messi** and the power of **Erling Haaland**. Sign that player up!

MARVELLOUS MBAPPÉ

MIDFIELD

DYNAMO DECLAN

The job of the midfield is to keep the ball and pass the ball. It may seem simple, but this can be where matches are won or lost. The midfield operates in the heart of the pitch and players need strong lungs because they do a lot of running. The different roles in midfield focus on gaining and keeping possession – and then making it count. The midfield often depends on the tactics, or formation, set out by the coach. The defensive, or holding, midfielder often plays in front of the defence to win possession; the box-to-box midfielder, such as **Declan Rice**, needs lots of energy to run between each penalty area (or box) to make a difference at both ends of the pitch; the attacking midfielder, such as **Alexia Putellas**, creates opportunities for the strikers; and the wide midfielder, also known as a winger, dribbles and crosses from the side of the pitch, or the wings. They are wing wizards!

DEFENCE

The job of the defence is to keep the ball out of the net. You can't lose if your opponents can't score! A good defence sticks together, ensuring there are no spaces for the opposition to create shooting opportunities. The centre-backs defend the area in front of goal by making interceptions and tackles. The best ones constantly communicate with each other and their right-back and left-back, who are known as full-backs. The full-backs defend the wide areas and keep opposition wingers away from dangerous areas. Some full-backs, such as **Reece James** and **Lucy Bronze**, are attacking threats and are known as wing-backs because they also play like wingers in supporting the attack. For that reason, the full-back has become one of the most important positions on the pitch. It's full on!

UNBREAKABLE BRONZE

GOALKEEPER

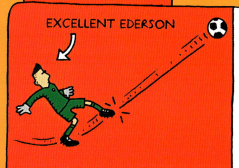

EXCELLENT EDERSON

The goalkeeper is the last line of defence: they stop shots. They are the only player who wears a different-coloured kit and who is allowed to catch the ball. Modern goalkeepers are also skilful with the ball at their feet: some, like **Alisson Becker**, patrol the edge of their box to snuff out chances, while others, like **Ederson**, can set up goals with their fabulous long passes. The best keepers just keep on keeping!

-CORE SKILLS-

While all players have some skills in common, such as running fast and passing the ball, there are specific key skills that are more helpful depending on the position on the pitch. Here we look at the most important skills for each of the four positions.

SHOOTING – FOR STRIKERS

If you are an attacking player, you need to know how to score. Goals win matches and are the most dramatic part of football. Goal-scorers become match-winners and heroes. But it isn't easy to score, especially when the defence are trying to stop you! One challenge is not just shooting with accuracy and power, but getting into position to take a shot in the first place. Ellen White, England women's team's all-time leading goal-scorer (with 52 goals), says scoring is all about being in the right place at the right time. Once in position, act quickly before an opponent tackles you. Go for goal!

HOW TO DO IT:

1. Check the position of the goalkeeper. Plant your non-kicking foot near the ball. Bring down your kicking foot.

2. Balance using your arms and upper body. Keep your head down and your eyes on the ball when striking.

3. Make contact with the middle of the ball. For extra power, follow through so the kick continues after the ball has been struck.

SUPER SKILLS

The best strikers, including **Erling Haaland**, **Vivianne Miedema** and **Kylian Mbappé**, all have these qualities:

★ **Composure** – they stay cool when faced with a chance to score, no matter the pressure.
★ **Technique** – they control the ball neatly and are skilled enough to shoot where they want.
★ **Vision** – they assess the surroundings, creating space and time to shoot.
★ **Speed** – they evade defenders and shoot before a tackle comes in.

HOW TO IMPROVE:

★ Practise shooting at a small target in an empty goal regularly.
★ Watch professional strikers to see how they find space away from defenders.
★ Practise trying to dribble or shoot past a goalkeeper.
★ Perfect your body position as you strike the ball.

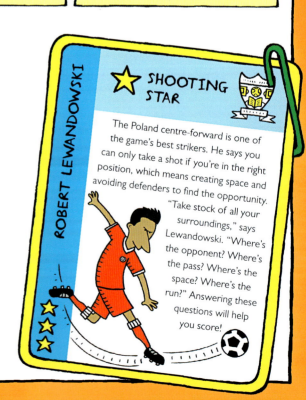

ROBERT LEWANDOWSKI

⭐ SHOOTING STAR

The Poland centre-forward is one of the game's best strikers. He says you can only take a shot if you're in the right position, which means creating space and avoiding defenders to find the opportunity. "Take stock of all your surroundings," says Lewandowski. "Where's the opponent? Where's the pass? Where's the space? Where's the run?" Answering these questions will help you score!

DRIBBLING – FOR MIDFIELDERS

The midfield is often the busiest part of the pitch, and so dribbling, or running with the ball at your feet, can help keep possession and get your team closer to the goal. Dribbling also allows you to get past opponents and set up passing or scoring opportunities for your team. The key skill required for dribbling is balance: the best players stay on their feet, even when challenged. They use their body shape to fool opponents, making them think they will go one way and in fact going the other. "You need to be able to change direction quickly – but you have to do it at the right moment," says Belgium winger Eden Hazard of his dribbling skills. Don't quibble – just dribble!

HOW TO DO IT:

1. Point your toes at the ground and use your laces to touch the ball.

2. Run, slowly at first, while moving the ball forward with your laces.

3. As your confidence increases, so should your speed. Next, try it while looking ahead so you can see where you are going.

SUPER SKILLS

The best dribblers, including **Lionel Messi**, **Allan Saint-Maximin** and **Beth Mead**, all have these qualities:

- ★ **Balance** – they move in all directions, using their whole body to confuse opponents.
- ★ **Control** – they keep the ball at their feet even when moving at speed.
- ★ **Co-ordination** – they tie everything together while assessing team-mates and avoiding tackles.
- ★ **Trickery** – they bamboozle defenders, by faking their direction of movement or disguising a run with their eyes.

HOW TO IMPROVE:

- ★ Place cones in a straight line and dribble between them.
- ★ Repeat these exercises but using your other foot.
- ★ Repeat these exercises using the instep, outside or the sole of the feet.
- ★ Repeat these exercises but now ask a friend to try and tackle you!

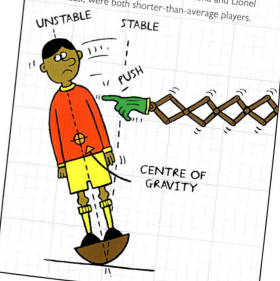

PHYSICS CORNER

Short people are usually better dribblers than tall ones because they find it easier to dart from side to side and not topple over. The centre of gravity of a shorter player moves less far from a stable position than the centre of gravity of a taller player when leaning at the same angle. Two of the greatest dribblers of all time, Diego Maradona and Lionel Messi, were both shorter-than-average players.

UNSTABLE STABLE

PUSH

CENTRE OF GRAVITY

TACKLING - FOR DEFENDERS

The best way to win back the ball from your opponents is to tackle them. You need to work hard and get your timing right – but be careful, because a mistimed tackle can lead to a free-kick, penalty or even a red card! Some coaches think the best chance of scoring is to shoot within ten seconds of winning the ball back – so the art of tackling, while a defensive action in itself, is often the launch pad for an attack and a goal. The best defenders anticipate where the ball is going, so making a tackle is another chance to gain possession if an interception has been missed. The Netherlands defender Virgil van Dijk says he shapes his body to encourage his opponent to move into a certain area before making a tackle. Van-tastic!

HOW TO DO IT:

1. Keep your eye on the ball as your opponent approaches.

2. Bend your knees so you are ready to tackle as soon as the opponent lets the ball move slightly away from them.

3. Strike the ball firmly with your stronger foot – be careful not to kick the opponent!

SUPER SKILLS

The best tacklers, including **Rúben Dias**, **Mapi León** and **William Saliba**, all have these qualities:

★ **Confidence** – they stay fully committed as anything less reduces their chances of success.
★ **Control** – they keep at least one foot on the ground so they and their opponent avoid injury.
★ **Timing** – they make the challenge at the right moment so as not to concede a free-kick.
★ **Anticipation** – they see where the opponent might go so they can get there first.

HOW TO IMPROVE:

★ Practise tackling different players from different angles (not from behind – that's illegal).
★ Work on timing and knowing the best time to make the tackle.
★ Two or more people dribble with their own ball. Tackle them while keeping your ball.
★ Play piggy-in-the-middle with the player in the middle trying to win back the ball.

PAOLO MALDINI

★ TACKLING TITAN

The Italian defender, known for his immaculate positioning and skills of anticipation, once said, "If I have to make a tackle then I have already made a mistake." His aim was always to be in the right place before he needed to tackle. Yes indeedy, Maldini!

SAVING – FOR GOALKEEPERS

The goalkeeper is the only specialist position on the pitch and your job is to stop goals by saving the ball. You can do this by catching, punching or blocking the ball – any way that stops the ball going into the goal. A top goalkeeper can be worth as many goals as a top striker – saving them is just as important as scoring them! But it's also hard to be a goalkeeper: you stand alone from the team in a different kit and are often blamed when a goal goes in (even if it's not your fault). Goalkeepers need to be mentally strong and able to bounce back after they let in a goal. Brazil goalkeeper Ederson describes the goalkeeper's life as intense, because one minute you can be a star and the next minute, a villain. You're either a hero, or a zero!

HOW TO DO IT:

1. Know exactly where you are in relation to the goal and make your body as large as possible (arms up, legs wide).

2. Bounce on your toes and narrow the angle to make the target smaller for the opponent.

3. Aim to catch the ball or push it away from the goal.

SUPER SKILLS

The best goalkeepers, including **Ederson**, **Mary Earps** and **Aaron Ramsdale**, all have these qualities:

★ **Good reactions** – they move quickly to respond to where the ball is going.
★ **Agility** – they bounce around and cover all areas of the goal, including top and bottom corners.
★ **Focus** – they concentrate for long periods, even when the ball is not near their goal.
★ **Resilience** – they stay composed even after conceding a goal or making a mistake.

HOW TO IMPROVE:

★ Sharpen your reactions by asking three players to take shots, one after the other in quick succession.
★ Ask someone to fire in crosses and attempt to catch them.
★ Have a striker run towards you in a one-on-one situation and stop them scoring.
★ Stand opposite another goalkeeper and try and kick the ball into each other's goal.

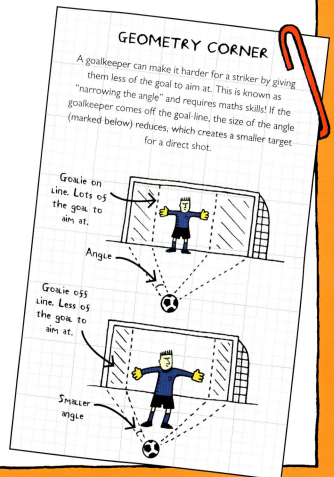

GEOMETRY CORNER

A goalkeeper can make it harder for a striker by giving them less of the goal to aim at. This is known as "narrowing the angle" and requires maths skills! If the goalkeeper comes off the goal-line, the size of the angle (marked below) reduces, which creates a smaller target for a direct shot.

Goalie on line. Lots of the goal to aim at.

Angle

Goalie off line. Less of the goal to aim at.

Smaller angle

-SET-PIECE-
SECRETS

A set-piece is when the ball is played from a corner, free kick, penalty or throw-in. Teams that practise set-piece routines can gain an important advantage. Here's how!

CORNERS

The attacking team gets a corner when the ball comes off a defending player and crosses the goal-line at either end of the pitch (without going in the goal). The defence needs to get in position to keep the corner kick away from goal.

THE RULES FOR TAKING A CORNER:

- The ball must be struck from the corner arc of the nearest corner from where it went out.
- Any player on the attacking team can take the corner.
- The ball must be stationary when struck.
- The corner flag must not be moved.
- When the corner is first struck, the opponents must be at least 10 yards away.

OLYMPIC CHAMPIONS

The first player to score direct from a corner was Argentine winger Cesáreo Onzari, whose goal came in a 2–1 win in 1924 against Uruguay. As Uruguay were reigning Olympic champions at the time, the act of scoring direct from a corner became known as an Olympico goal.

CHANCE OF SCORING:
3 per cent when the ball is in play after a corner

DIFFERENT CORNER TACTICS

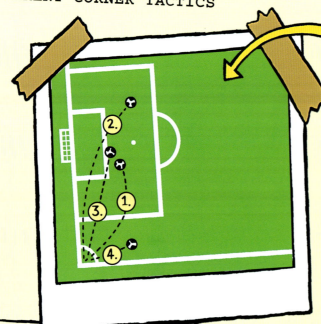

1. **In-swinging:** Striking the ball so that it curls towards the goal. (A kick on the right side of the ball curls it to the left, and vice versa).

2. **Out-swinging:** An out-swinging corner curls away from goal and is harder for the goalkeeper to catch, leading to more efforts on goal.

3. **Straight:** Striking the ball in the middle and with pace. This relies on attackers anticipating where the ball will end up.

4. **Short:** A short corner is often taken quickly and can result in a cross coming in from another angle, potentially surprising the defence.

THROW-INS

A throw-in is the method used to put the ball back on the field when it goes off the side of the pitch. The aim is to keep possession after the throw.

THE RULES FOR A THROW-IN:

- The throw must be taken from where the ball went out.
- The ball must come from behind the thrower's head and over it, held by both hands.
- The thrower must have at least part of each foot on or outside of the line.
- The defending team must stay 2 metres away from the line.
- Goalkeepers can't pick up a ball from a throw-in.
- Goals cannot be scored directly from a throw-in.
- Players can't be offside from a throw-in.

TYPES OF THROW-IN

REDS THROWN A LIFELINE

Before Liverpool started using a throw-in coach in 2019, their rate of keeping possession from throw-ins was 45 per cent. After they hired Thomas Grønnemark, a former world-record holder for the longest throw-in, it went up to 68 per cent!

NUMBER OF THROW-INS PER MATCH: 45 on average

1. <u>Long throw</u>: If you can throw the ball into the penalty area, you will put opponents under pressure – and the throw-in can become as dangerous as a corner.

2. <u>Fast throw</u>: Taking the throw quickly, before defenders are in position, is an ideal way to launch counter-attacks.

3. <u>Clever throw</u>: Throwing the ball in a flat line can surprise targets, allow you to keep possession under pressure and start attacks from unexpected areas.

FREE KICKS

Free kicks are awarded in the event of foul play. A direct free kick allows you to shoot on goal and score without anyone else touching the ball. An indirect free kick is when another player has to touch the ball before a goal can be scored.

DIRECT FREE KICKS ARE AWARDED FOR:

- Handball
- Holding an opponent
- Careless or reckless play
- Spitting or biting at someone

INDIRECT FREE KICKS ARE AWARDED FOR:

- Blocking an opponent
- Dangerous play
- Rude language to officials

THE RULES FOR TAKING A FREE KICK:

- All free kicks are taken from the place where the offence occurred.
- The ball must be stationary and, for indirect free kicks, the kicker must not touch the ball again until it has touched another player.
- All opponents must remain at least 10 yards from the ball, unless they are on their own goal-line between the goalposts.
- Players are allowed to feint to take a free kick to confuse opponents.

FREE KICK TACTICS

MESSI MASTERCLASS

Argentine Lionel Messi is the most prolific free-kick taker in football, having scored over 20 direct free kicks in the last five years. England midfielder James Ward-Prowse is second. Even though free kicks are harder, Ward-Prowse says he prefers taking them to penalties!

CHANCE OF SCORING: 6 per cent (from direct free kicks that are shots on goal)

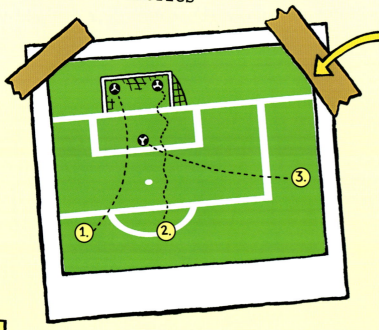

1. Curling free kick: The challenge is to hit the ball around — or sometimes over — the defensive wall and have enough swerve on the ball to hit the target.

2. Knuckleball free kick: The bottom of the ball is struck without spin so the ball generates natural movement through the air, so it could swerve unexpectedly to wrong-foot the goalkeeper.

3. Crossed free kick: A set-piece specialist swings a curling cross into a dangerous position that makes it hard for the defence to clear.

PENALTIES

A penalty kick is awarded if a defending player commits a direct free-kick foul against an attacking player inside their penalty area. The attacking team chooses a player to take a shot from the penalty spot, with just the goalkeeper to beat.

THE RULES FOR TAKING A PENALTY:

- The ball must be stationary on the penalty spot.
- The players – other than the kicker and goalkeeper – must be outside the penalty area and the D.
- The player taking the penalty kick must kick the ball forwards.
- When the ball is kicked, the goalkeeper must have at least part of one foot touching, or in line with, the goal-line.
- The kicker must not play the ball again until it has touched another player.

CHANCE OF SCORING:
78 per cent

PENALTY SHOOT-OUTS

A penalty shoot-out is when each team alternately kicks five penalties to determine the winner of a tied knock-out match. It gets very tense – and dramatic!

SECRETS TO PENALTY SUCCESS

1. Take your time: Studies show that the players who react quickest to the referee's whistle to take the penalty are most likely to miss. Always take an extra breath!

1.

2.

2. Practise your strategy: You can aim penalties high or low, kick with accuracy or power – just work out beforehand what you plan to do. And whatever you decide, practise!

3.

3. Think positive: Goalkeepers may try to distract you from the penalty. Keep your head up and remember your practice penalties; mark out the correct run-up, and don't change your mind about where you are aiming. Most of all, think positive: if you think you are going to miss, you might just do that!

-ANATOMY OF A-
FOOTBALLER

It's a game with a limb in the name! Here we describe the roles of, and risks to, different body parts when playing football.

FOREHEAD

The preferred point of contact for balls arriving above shoulder height. But be careful! Heading a ball can really hurt. Also, doctors have shown that frequent heading may cause brain damage in old age because of how these collisions shake the brain. The FA forbids Under-11s from heading the ball in training, and eleven- and twelve-year-olds are only allowed a maximum of five headers in training a month. Foreheaders? No, five!

NOSE

The nose has two functions – breathing and smelling. Both have relevance on the pitch. Breathing is the process in which oxygen (in the air) is brought to the lungs. Athletes are advised to breathe through their noses, rather than their mouths, since it allows more oxygen to be absorbed by the lungs. Oxygen is what gives the body energy and footballers need as much of it as they can get! The nose is also used to smell, which is why Italy defender Leo Bonucci once ate garlic sweets before a big match. He wanted to distract his opponents with pongy breath. Reek!

TOES

When it comes to kicking a ball, the toes are first in line and as a result they suffer from many nasty conditions. These include black toe, when the skin under the nail bleeds, turning the toe black or purple. Another common complaint is claw toe, where the four small toes curl in rather than lying flat, often a result of wearing too-tight boots from a young age. Claws of the game!

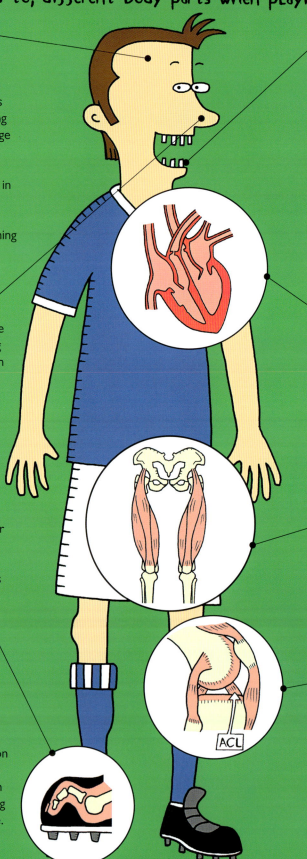

TEETH

The purpose of teeth is for biting food, not players, although tell that to Uruguay forward Luis Suárez, who has bitten three different opponents and been banned every time. Yet – thanks to their prominent position in the front of the face – teeth are often innocent victims of the rough and tumble of play. Many players have had teeth knocked out during games, including Callum Wilson, Mikel Arteta and Peter Crouch. Fangs for the memories, guys!

HEART

The heart pumps blood – containing oxygen absorbed by the lungs – around the body, providing muscles with energy. As you increase physical activity, the heart pumps faster. The average person's heart beats 60–100 times per minute. During a game, footballers will average around 170 heartbeats per minute. Beat that!

QUADRICEPS

The quadriceps, or quads, are muscles at the front of the thigh that provide most of the power when a footballer kicks a ball. Brazil defender Roberto Carlos, best-known for his cannon-like free kicks, had huge quads. In-quad-ible!

KNEE

Twist your knee in a tackle and you may tear the anterior cruciate ligament, or ACL, the tissue in the knee that connects the thigh bone on top to the shin bone below. It is one of the most feared injuries because it can take from six months to a year to recuperate from. Dutch defender Virgil van Dijk was out for nine months when he tore his. AC-heLL!

BRAIN

The brain is in control of decision-making, an important skill in football (and life). Some top clubs, including Liverpool, attach electrodes to players' heads during training in order to measure brain activity during key moments, such as just before a free kick. Scientists use this data to help the players improve decision-making, reaction times and concentration. Brain-iacs!

SKIN

The millions of sweat glands on the surface of the skin get plenty of use during a game as the body works to stay cool. Footballers will usually sweat between one and two litres of water (or four to eight glasses) per game. Sodden!

BUTTOCKS

The gluteus maximus – the main muscle in both buttocks – is the biggest muscle in the body. Its main function is to keep the body upright. Footballers are given exercises to strengthen this crucial muscle, because players with strong glutes can push their opponent away with their bum, creating space to control the ball and escape tight spaces. Players like Belgium's Eden Hazard and Scotland's John McGinn use their glutes to maximum effect. Gluteus maximus indeed!

CALF

A footballer uses the calf muscles to push forward when they run, and also to propel them in the air when they jump. Fast dribblers such as England's Jack Grealish have well-developed calf muscles. Springy!

HEEL

The Achilles tendon joins the heel bone to the calf muscle, and acts like a lever between the leg and the foot so is essential for kicking. It is easy to tear and it can take months to recuperate from. Tender tendon!

EYE

Top footballers tend to have an above-average ability to see details in the distance (like a ball being kicked on the other side of the pitch), to detect objects against a background and to change their focus between near and far. Footballers regularly exercise their eyes to keep their vision in top condition, with training exercises like kicking a ball and naming a colour they can see to their side, or putting a toothpick in a straw while focusing on something else. Visionaries!

HAIR

Footballers put a lot of care into their hair. They believe if they look good, they will feel good, and therefore will perform better. One study showed that male players with no hair or short hair are almost twice as likely to head the ball on target. USA even have a barber travel with them to make sure their players look sharp in international matches. Short (full) back and sides!

HAMSTRING

The hamstring muscles at the back of the thigh counter-balance the quadriceps. Straining a hamstring is the most common football injury (making up 12 per cent of all injuries) and happens when the muscle is stretched, often when players are sprinting or changing pace. France winger Ousmane Dembélé and England defender John Stones both struggled with hamstring injuries. What a strain!

FOOT

There are 26 bones in the foot, but the ones footballers are most concerned about are the metatarsals: these are the five long thin bones in the middle of each foot. They are most at risk of injury because, unlike the toe bones at the end of the foot, they cannot flex out of the way. Brittle!

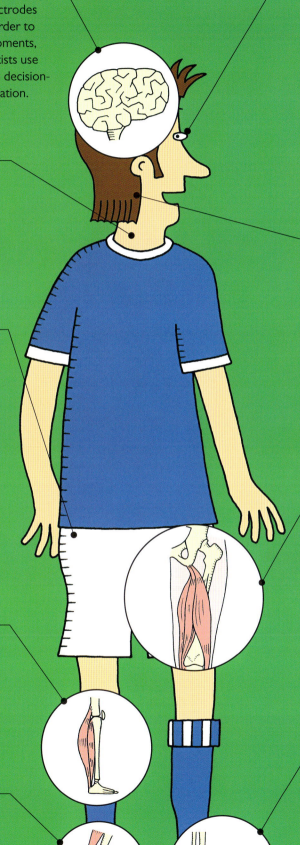

-SHIRTS-

Football shirts were originally made from heavy cotton, with long sleeves, a collar, and buttons or laces at the neck. Let's take a look at how they evolved into a modern, high-tech sporting uniform.

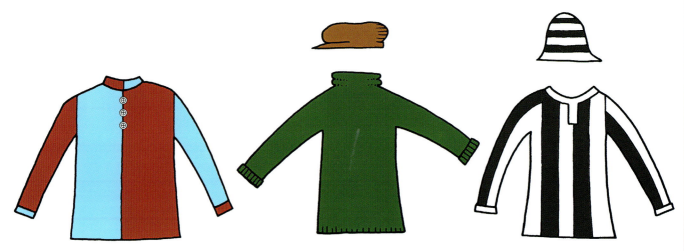

1. Aston Villa, 1888

In the English league's first season in 1888, three teams wore plain colours, four wore vertical stripes and five teams, including Villa, wore "quarters", with each arm a different colour.

2. Goalkeepers, 1910s–70s

From 1909, keepers had to wear a different colour from their team-mates. Most wore green. Because they moved less, their jerseys were warmer, made out of wool, often with roll necks.

3. Dick, Kerr Ladies, 1922

Plain colours and vertical stripes dominated football's early decades. The successful women's team Dick, Kerr Ladies had matching striped bonnets for their hair.

4. Hungary, 1954

Footballers from warm countries started to wear shirts made from lighter materials with simpler designs and round or V-neck collars. A classic example is this Hungary top.

5. Netherlands, 1988

In the 1980s, advances in textile technology enabled clubs and national teams, such as the Netherlands, to print fancy patterns in fancy colours on their shirts. Shirts became fashion items worn by fans.

6. Italy, 2021

In the twenty-first century, shirts used lighter and less absorbent materials to improve player performance. This Italy jersey weighed only 72g, about the same weight as an egg. Cracking!

THE MODERN SHIRT: STITCH BY STITCH

Material

Shirts are normally made from synthetic materials such as nylon. This makes them hard to rip, helps sweat to evaporate quicker and makes them lighter than natural fibres.

Brand

The logo of the shirt manufacturer is usually on the chest. The three most popular shirt brands in football – Nike, Adidas and Puma – originally started off making shoes.

Sponsor

Clubs receive money from companies in exchange for letting the company advertise on their shirt. The bigger the club, the more money they charge.

Stars

Some national teams and clubs display one or more stars next to their badge, to denote important victories like a World Cup or a Champions League win. The trend was started in 1958 by Juventus, who used a star to represent their tenth Serie A title.

Badge

The club badge, or crest, is an emblem that represents the club. It often includes symbols from heraldry, such as roses, eagles and lions, or that reflect local history and geography, such as hammers, ships and water.

FRONT

MEGAGLOBAL CORPORATION

Tournament logo

Tournaments such as the Premier League, the Champions League and the World Cup have their logo on the shirt sleeve.

Name

Most footballers tend to have their surnames on the backs of their shirts, but they can also use their first name or a nickname, as long as it is approved by the competition they are playing in. Reasons given for using a first name are a family dispute, having a very common surname or having a very long one! Brazilians almost always use first names or nicknames.

Font

Some competitions, such as the Premier League, insist that every club uses the same style of letters and numbers, called a font, on the back. But in cup competitions, clubs can use their own fonts, which are sometimes a bit wacky!

Number

Shirt numbers were used in England for the first time in 1928: one team wore 1–11, and the other 12–22. Later, the tradition was established that the goalkeeper wears 1, and the numbers ascend as the positions go through defence, midfield and attack, with 9, 10 and 11 being the forwards.

BACK

BELLOS

10

-KIT-

Accessories all areas! Here are ten items of specialized clothing that footballers wear — but not all at the same time!

1. Sports hijab
The hijab is a headscarf worn by some Muslim women to cover their heads. FIFA has allowed footballers to wear hijabs since 2014.

2. Headband
Players wear them to keep their hair out of their eyes. Can be as thin as a piece of string or thicker like a ribbon.

3. Armband
The team captain wears an armband. If the captain is sent off, another player puts on the armband.

4. Gloves
Goalkeepers wear gloves to get a better grip on the ball and to protect their hands. The other players sometimes wear gloves in winter games to keep warm.

5. Sports bra
Provides support and comfort to help performance.

6. GPS tracking vest
These vests measure speed and distance travelled. Coaches and players use this information so they know how and where to improve performance.

7. Shorts
A century ago shorts went almost to the knee. They became very short about 50 years ago and are now long again. That's fashion!

8. Shinpads
Football borrowed the idea of protective shin guards from cricket. Howzat!

9. Socks
The Laws of the Game require socks to be worn high to cover the shin pads. They are also part of the team's colours. Players who find long sports socks uncomfortably tight often cut holes in the backs of them to relieve the pressure.

10. Grip socks
These are short socks with grip pads to stop feet slipping inside boots. Some players cut off the foot part of their official socks so they can wear grip socks in their shoes, while wearing the shin parts of the official socks on their shins.

-BOOTS-

The earliest footballers wore sturdy leather boots which rose above the ankle. The modern boot, however, is a precision piece of technology with several carefully designed elements.

BARE TRUTH

Kicking a football barefoot will make the ball go faster than if you kick it wearing a boot. (Although it will be more painful!) This is because the bare foot is a more rigid surface than a boot, and the ankle can flex more.

1. Studs
Studs are small pieces of metal or plastic attached to the sole of a boot that help the player grip the turf. For playing on wet ground, boots usually have metal studs: two in the heel and four in the forefoot. For playing on hard ground, the studs are usually plastic: four in the back and up to nine in the front. Front studs help a player go faster; back ones help them slow down.

2. Sole
The sole of the boot is designed to be stiff, which helps the player to go faster.

3. Material
Boots are made from synthetic leather, which absorbs less water than real leather and is lighter.

4. Surface
Some boots have a sticky surface, while others are scaly, in order to increase the time that the boot and ball are in contact during a kick. An extra half a millisecond's contact can help the player control the spin and direction of the kick.

5. Laces
Most footballers prefer laces, because laces are the best way to adjust a boot so it fits the foot. Others prefer laceless boots that have a smooth area on the top of the boot, which can help with ball control.

6. Colour
A colourful boot doesn't make you a better striker. But it makes for a more striking shoe! Sports brands provide famous players with snazzily coloured boots as a way to reach fans, who they hope will buy versions of these boots.

-THE BALL-

Circle time! For centuries footballs were inflated pig's bladders bound in animal skin. They are now technological marvels. Let's sphere it for the game's glorious globes!

RUBBER SOLUTION

Rebecca Lindon's job in the 1850s was to make footballs by blowing into pigs' bladders, tying their ends and enclosing the bladders in leather. When she died after catching a disease from an infected bladder, her distraught husband, Richard, replaced the bladder with rubber, a new material in the UK. The result was the first modern ball.

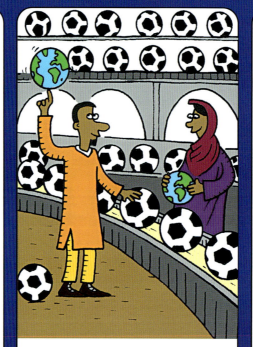

BALL FACTORY

The city of Sialkot in Pakistan has for decades been the world centre for football production, responsible for somewhere between 40 and 70 per cent of the world's footballs. The city provided the balls for the World Cup in 2014, 2018 and 2022.

BALL HAUL STANDS TALL

Mexican businessman Rodrigo Romero has collected 1,230 footballs, which according to the *Guinness Book of World Records* is the largest collection in the world.

-BALL OF FAME-
SPHERICAL STARS OF THE WORLD CUP

Telstar 1970
Most famous ball

Jabulani 2010
Most wobbly ball

Brazuca 2014
Most propellory ball

Al Rihla 2022
Most triangly ball

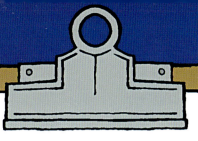

THE SEVEN TESTS

Leagues and tournaments need to make sure they use balls with the same physical characteristics. Otherwise it wouldn't be fair. For a ball to be certified as "FIFA quality", it must pass these seven factory tests:

 1. Size
A Circumference and Sphericity Measuring System, or CSM, measures the ball at 4,500 points to make sure it is the right size.

 2. Shape
The CSM measures the ball at 4,500 points to make sure it is a sphere.

 3. Bounce
The ball is dropped from 2 metres onto a steel plate. It must rebound to a height of between 133 cm and 155 cm.

 4. Water absorption
A ball must not absorb more than 10 per cent of its weight in water after 250 compressions in a ball-squashing machine half-filled with water. The device has a crusher that descends from above to squash the ball and a mechanism on the side to turn it.

 5. Weight
The ball is weighed using electronic scales. It must weigh between 420g and 445g.

 6. Pressure loss
Pressure is measured over a 72-hour period. If the ball loses more than 20 per cent of its pressure it will fail.

 7. Shape retention
The ball is shot 2,000 times at a steel plate at 31 mph in a contraption that consists of a cannon and a chute to catch the rebounds. If the ball doesn't maintain its size, weight and shape it will fail.

-GALLERY OF-
THE GREATS

Welcome to our treasury of talent-celebrating heroes who improved the game on or off the pitch. ALL hail these record-breakers and change-makers!

Pelé
The king of football

Pelé was only seventeen when his six goals helped Brazil win the 1958 World Cup. Victories in 1962 and 1970 meant Pelé, the first player to score over a thousand goals, was the first (and so far, only) male player to win three World Cups.

Marta
World Cup legend

A six-time World Player of the Year winner, between 2006 and 2018, Brazil's Marta is the first player to score at five different World Cups, and is the leading scorer of any player at World Cups.

Pelé is just a nickname. His real name was Edson Arantes do Nascimento and he was named after the lightbulb inventor Thomas Edison!

Cristiano Ronaldo
Portuguese perfection

Portugal's greatest player has scored more goals in international football than any other male player. Ronaldo is also Real Madrid's all-time leading scorer with an incredible 451 goals in 438 matches between 2009 and 2018.

Ronaldo celebrates goals by jumping up with his arms out and shouting "Siuuuu!" adapted from "si", meaning "yes" in Spanish. He began doing it in 2013 to connect to the Real Madrid fans.

Goal celebrations forbidden!

Amadeo Carrizo
Transformed goalkeeper role

The Argentine goalkeeper, who won seven league titles for River Plate in the 1950s, was the first to stand outside his area, use his feet to keep out through-balls and dribble to launch attacks.

Lily Parr
Prolific and powerful striker

Parr was the star striker of Dick, Kerr Ladies team, the female team from Preston who were best in the world in 1919. Her kick was so hard it was claimed that one of her shots broke a male goalkeeper's arm!

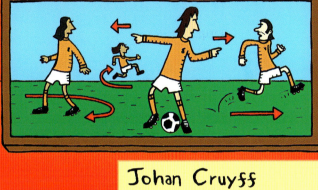

Johan Cruyff
Tactical genius

As a Dutch player and then a coach, in the 1970s Cruyff pioneered a successful attacking style of football involving players switching positions. He was highly influential at Ajax, Barcelona and the Netherlands and many successful coaches still use his theories.

Samuel Eto'o
Incredible Indomitable Lion

Striker Eto'o, who was named African Player of the Year four times, has scored more goals than any other player in the Africa Cup of Nations, a tournament he helped Cameroon win in 2000 and 2002.

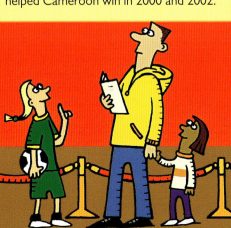

Stanley Matthews
The Wizard of Dribble

England's brilliant dribbler and crosser, and the first-ever winner of the Ballon d'Or in 1956, Matthews was still playing in the top division when he was 50.

Hey, did you know that Cruyff unveiled a new trick, called the Cruyff Turn, during the Netherlands' 1974 World Cup match against Sweden?

Diego Maradona
Dribbling danger man

Maradona single-handedly inspired Argentina to success in the 1986 World Cup. One of his goals, a solo dribble in the quarter-final against England, has been voted the greatest ever scored.

Alfredo Di Stéfano
Real international star

Argentine Di Stéfano scored in the first five European Cup finals for Real Madrid between 1956 and 1960, and played for three different national teams: Argentina, Colombia and Spain.

Christine Sinclair
Record-breaking scorer

Sinclair broke the all-time record for most international goals when she scored goal number 185 for Canada in a 2020 win over Saint Kitts and Nevis. No one has more!

Mia Hamm
USA pioneer

Hamm is USA's greatest-ever player, winning the 1991 and 1999 World Cups, and the 1996 and 2004 Olympics to propel the women's game to a huge audience. Nike named a building after her at their American HQ.

Sinclair is an incredible scorer! Did you know most of her Canada goals were scored on a Wednesday?

George Weah
Striker turned president

The first African winner of the Ballon d'Or in 1995, Weah understood how football could change lives and in 2018 was elected president of his country, Liberia.

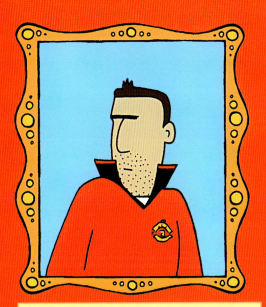

Megan Rapinoe
Champion activist

Rapinoe won consecutive World Cup titles in 2015 and 2019 with the USA women's team, at the same time as campaigning for racial and gender equality.

Eric Cantona
Premier League's foreign superstar

The French forward, a five-time English league title winner with Leeds United (once) and Manchester United (four times) between 1992 and 1997, encouraged other English clubs to buy talented foreign players.

Ada Hegerberg
Striker with impact

A prolific and speedy striker, Norway's Hegerberg won six Champions League titles with Olympique Lyonnais Féminin, including a 16-minute hat-trick in 2019's 4–1 final win over Barcelona.

Lionel Messi
Brilliant Barcelona inspiration

Winner of a record-breaking seven Ballons d'Or, Messi is arguably the greatest passer, dribbler and scorer of all time. He inspired Argentina to success in the 2022 World Cup.

Hegerberg quit the Norway national team in protest at the unequal opportunities granted to female players. She refused to compete in the 2019 World Cup to make the world better for the next generation of female Norwegian players. It's Ada's way or Norway!

-THE GAME-
QUIZ

1. **Who wrote the first set of rules for football in 1848?**

   a) King Henry VIII
   b) A group of students at Cambridge University
   c) Two players in a Sheffield cricket club
   d) William Shakespeare

2. **From which one of the following situations can a player be called offside?**

   a) Goal kick
   b) Free kick
   c) Corner
   d) Throw-in

3. **What is the name given to a goal scored directly from a corner?**

   a) Olympico
   b) Cornerama
   c) Sombrero
   d) Elastico

4. **Match the situation to the percentage chances of scoring:**

Situation	Chance of scoring
1) Corner	a) 78 per cent
2) Penalty	b) 3 per cent
3) Direct free kick	c) 6 per cent

5. **The gluteus maximus is the biggest muscle in the body. Where is it?**

   a) Buttock
   b) Upper arm
   c) Thigh
   d) Chest

6. **Which team, in 1958, began the trend of putting a star above their team badge on a shirt to denote a famous victory?**

   a) Manchester United
   b) Real Madrid
   c) Hungary
   d) Juventus

7. **What rule concerning socks appears in The Laws of the Game?**

   a) They must be washed before every game.
   b) There must be no holes in them.
   c) They must be worn high to cover shin-pads.
   d) They must be folded down below the knee.

8. **Which country in the world makes the most footballs?**

   a) Bhutan
   b) Turkmenistan
   c) Kazakhstan
   d) Pakistan

9. **Which of these statements about Brazil forward Marta is true?**

   a) She was the first player to score in seven World Cups.
   b) She was crowned World Player of the Year eight times.
   c) She has scored the winning goal in three World Cup finals.
   d) She is the all-time leading scorer in World Cups.

10. **In what African country was former Ballon d'Or winner George Weah voted president in 2017?**

   a) Senegal
   b) Lesotho
   c) Liberia
   d) Mali

Answers: 1. b, 2. b, 3. a, 4. 1) b, 2) a, 3) c, 5. a, 6. d, 7. c, 8. d, 9. d, 10. c

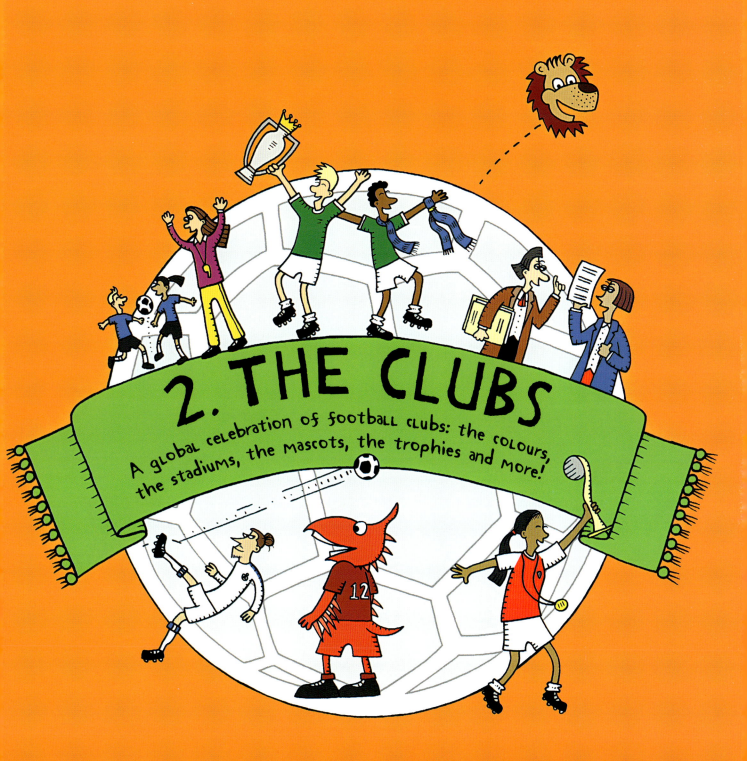

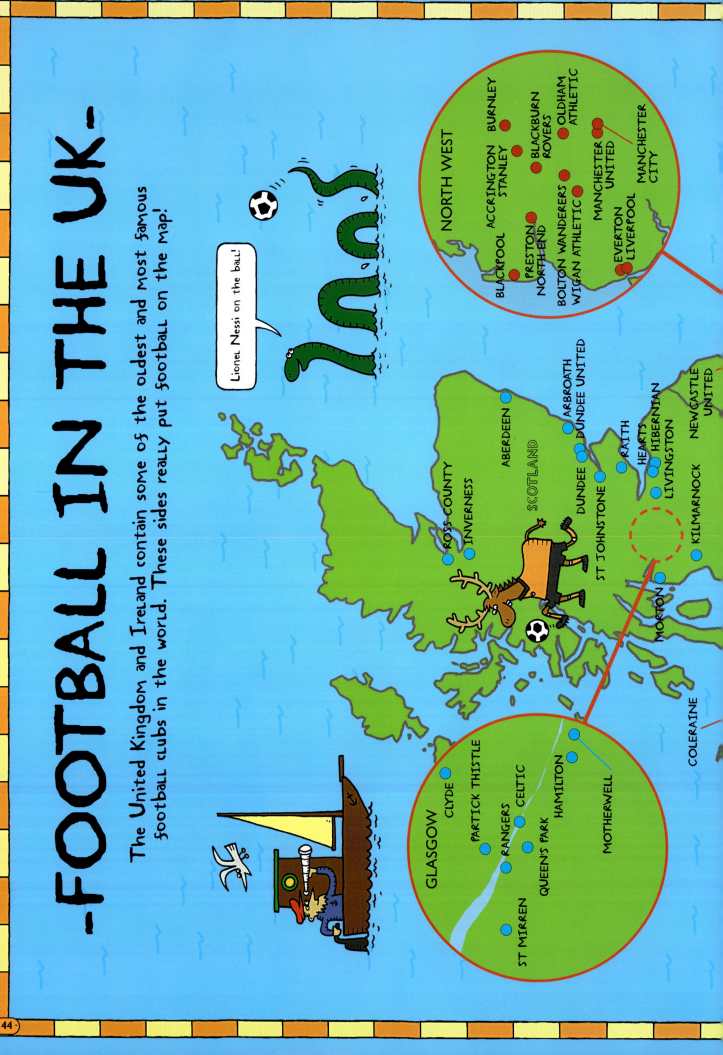

It's time for a fact-filled tour around the UK's most fascinating clubs.

Arsenal
- Nicknamed The Gunners as the club was founded by workers at the Royal Arsenal weapons factory.
- Most successful club in English women's football.
- Club with the longest ongoing run in the top division, it's been ever-present since 1920.

Aston Villa
- Have supplied more players to the England team than any other club.
- Team supported by Prince William as following them is an "emotional roller coaster".
- First club to sell an English player for £100m, when Jack Grealish joined Manchester City in 2021.

Cardiff City
- One of four Welsh clubs, with Swansea, Newport and Wrexham, to play in the English league system.
- Only non-English team to win the FA Cup – in 1927.
- New owner Vincent Tan changed the kit in 2012 from red to blue, but fans protested so they switched back after three seasons.

Celtic
- Set up in 1887 by an Irish priest to help the Irish immigrant community in Glasgow.
- First British team to win the European Cup in 1967 – with thirteen players born within 10 miles of the club stadium.
- Only European team to win nine titles in a row on two separate occasions.

Chelsea
- Stamford Bridge stadium is owned by a fans' group called Chelsea Pitch Owners.
- Women's team has won a record four league and FA Cup doubles in the same season.
- Sold for £1 in 1982 and sold again in 2022 for £2.5 billion.

Everton
- Nicknamed The Toffees as two toffee shops were near the stadium when it was founded in 1878.
- Have spent more time in the top division than any other English team.
- Goodison Park stadium was the first in England to have dugouts, floodlights and undersoil heating.

Fulham
- The oldest pro club in London play at Craven Cottage stadium, the oldest ground in London.
- George Best spent one season at Fulham in 1976.
- Changed division five times running between 2018 and 2022 after three promotions and two relegations from the Premier League.

Leeds United
- First called Leeds City, but were expelled from the league and re-formed as United in 1919.
- Wore blue-and-white and blue-and-yellow shirts, before using all-white kit in 1960s to copy Real Madrid.
- Fans renamed pub next to stadium the Bielsa after ex-coach Marcelo Bielsa.

Leicester City
- Known as The Foxes as Leicestershire is considered the origin of UK fox-hunting.
- Won the 2016 Premier League against all odds, after being tipped for relegation.
- Surprise winners of the 2021 FA Cup final, their first Cup success after losing previous four finals.

Lewes Women
- First gender-equal club in the world; spending same amount on men's and women's teams.
- Have played at the Dripping Pan stadium since 1885.
- Owned fully by fans and run not for profit, but to support the local community.

Liverpool
- Fans' anthem "You'll Never Walk Alone" originally written for 1945 musical Carousel.
- Former coach Bill Shankly changed kit to all-red in 1964 to make team more intimidating.
- England's best club in Europe, with four European Cups and two Champions Leagues.

Manchester City

- Only English club ever relegated with a positive goal difference in 1938.
- Owners City Football Group also own clubs in Australia, India, Japan, Belgium, USA and China.
- First team to win the top division with 100 points, in 2018, with a record 32 wins.

Manchester United

- Originally called Newton Heath until renamed Manchester United in 1902.
- Former coach Sir Alex Ferguson won a record thirteen Premier League titles.
- Have gone over 4,000 games with at least one player from their youth academy in the squad.

Newcastle United

- Famous for black-and-white striped shirts, but for their first two years wore red-and-white shirts.
- Newcastle fans were the first to wear replica shirts at matches in 1973.
- One of the richest clubs in the world after a Saudi Arabia-based fund bought the club in 2021.

Nottingham Forest

- In 1886, Forest donated their kit to help Arsenal, hence why Arsenal plays in red.
- Signed the first £1m player, striker Trevor Francis, who scored the 1979 European Cup final winner.
- City Ground stadium is 300 yards away from Notts County stadium, the two closest stadiums in UK.

Plymouth Argyle

- Most southerly *and* westerly club in England; the only one called Argyle.
- Famously beat a Santos team from Brazil that included Pelé 3–2 in a 1973 friendly.
- The largest city with a club that has never played in the top division.

Preston North End

- Moved to north side of town shortly after their formation in 1863, adding "North End" to their name.
- First team to win the football league, in 1888; won league and FA Cup double one year later.
- Greatest player, Tom Finney, was known as the Preston Plumber as he had a second job.

Rangers

- Founded by rowing fans and named after the Swindon Rangers rugby team.
- First club in the world to win more than 50 league titles.
- Reached the 2022 Europa League final, only losing to Eintracht Frankfurt after a penalty shoot-out.

Shamrock Rovers

- Founded in 1901 on Dublin's Shamrock Avenue, hence the name.
- Provided more players for the Republic of Ireland team than any other club.
- Had a second star added above their club badge in 2022 to mark winning league title number 20 – each star represents ten titles.

Sheffield Wednesday

- Named as Wednesday was a half-day off work, so workers set up a club.
- Nicknamed The Owls after they moved their stadium to Owlerton in 1899.
- Striker David Hirst struck the Premier League's hardest recorded shot, at 114 mph, against Arsenal in 1999.

Tottenham Hotspur

- Named after Harry Hotspur, the English knight whose victory over the Scots in 1402 won him the Tottenham borough.
- New stadium doubles up as a venue for American football matches.
- Striker Harry Kane, England's top scorer, won 2018 World Cup Golden Boot while at Spurs.

West Ham

- Based in East London but called West Ham as they're in the west part of Newham.
- Had three players who won England's first World Cup in 1966, including hat-trick hero Geoff Hurst and captain Bobby Moore.
- Known as the Academy of Football due to excellent youth development.

Wolverhampton Wanderers

- Legendary captain Billy Wright was the first player to reach 100 caps for England.
- One of only three teams to win all four divisions in English football.
- Announced new signing Diego Costa in 2022 by surrounding the player with a pack of real wolves.

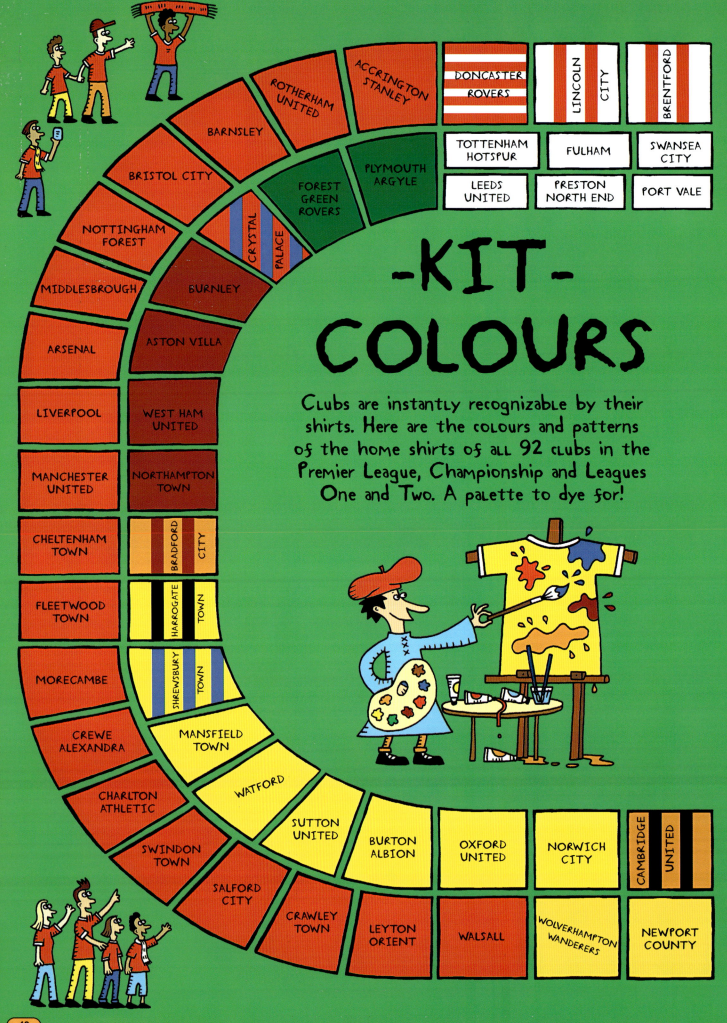

-KIT- COLOURS

Clubs are instantly recognizable by their shirts. Here are the colours and patterns of the home shirts of all 92 clubs in the Premier League, Championship and Leagues One and Two. A palette to dye for!

DONCASTER ROVERS

LINCOLN CITY

BRENTFORD

TOTTENHAM HOTSPUR

FULHAM

SWANSEA CITY

LEEDS UNITED

PRESTON NORTH END

PORT VALE

ACCRINGTON STANLEY

ROTHERHAM UNITED

BARNSLEY

BRISTOL CITY

NOTTINGHAM FOREST

MIDDLESBROUGH

ARSENAL

LIVERPOOL

MANCHESTER UNITED

CHELTENHAM TOWN

FLEETWOOD TOWN

MORECAMBE

CREWE ALEXANDRA

CHARLTON ATHLETIC

SWINDON TOWN

PLYMOUTH ARGYLE

FOREST GREEN ROVERS

CRYSTAL PALACE

BURNLEY

ASTON VILLA

WEST HAM UNITED

NORTHAMPTON TOWN

BRADFORD CITY

HARROGATE TOWN

SHREWSBURY TOWN

MANSFIELD TOWN

WATFORD

SUTTON UNITED

BURTON ALBION

OXFORD UNITED

NORWICH CITY

SALFORD CITY

CRAWLEY TOWN

LEYTON ORIENT

WALSALL

WOLVERHAMPTON WANDERERS

NEWPORT COUNTY

CAMBRIDGE UNITED

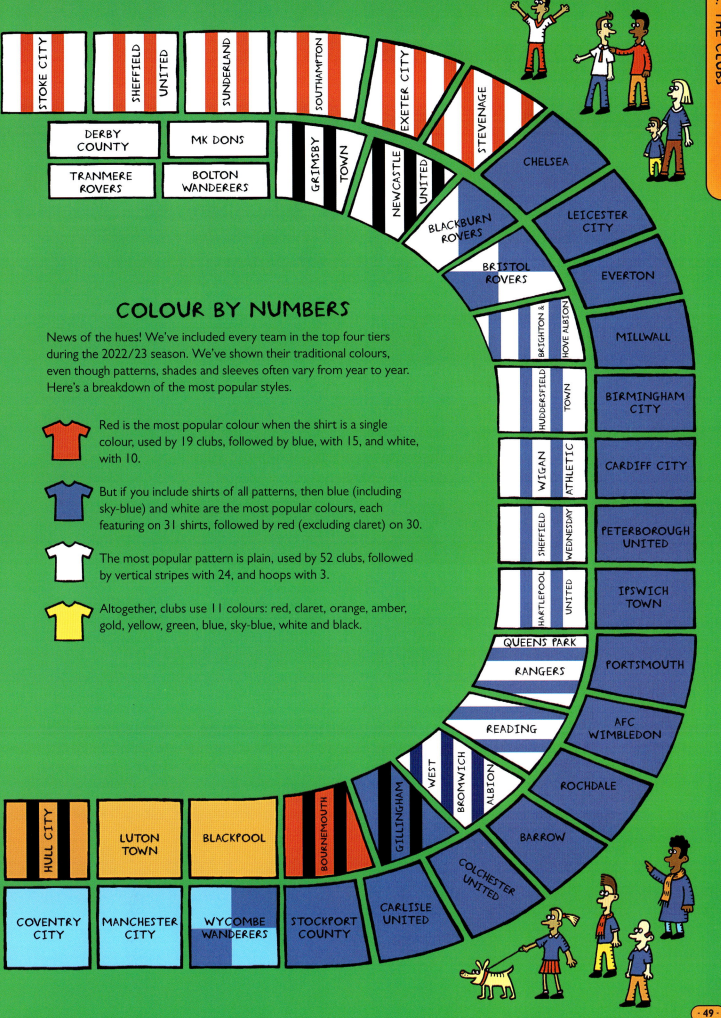

COLOUR BY NUMBERS

News of the hues! We've included every team in the top four tiers during the 2022/23 season. We've shown their traditional colours, even though patterns, shades and sleeves often vary from year to year. Here's a breakdown of the most popular styles.

Red is the most popular colour when the shirt is a single colour, used by 19 clubs, followed by blue, with 15, and white, with 10.

But if you include shirts of all patterns, then blue (including sky-blue) and white are the most popular colours, each featuring on 31 shirts, followed by red (excluding claret) on 30.

The most popular pattern is plain, used by 52 clubs, followed by vertical stripes with 24, and hoops with 3.

Altogether, clubs use 11 colours: red, claret, orange, amber, gold, yellow, green, blue, sky-blue, white and black.

STOKE CITY

SHEFFIELD UNITED

SUNDERLAND

SOUTHAMPTON

EXETER CITY

STEVENAGE

DERBY COUNTY

MK DONS

TRANMERE ROVERS

BOLTON WANDERERS

GRIMSBY TOWN

NEWCASTLE UNITED

CHELSEA

LEICESTER CITY

BLACKBURN ROVERS

EVERTON

BRISTOL ROVERS

MILLWALL

BRIGHTON & HOVE ALBION

HUDDERSFIELD TOWN

BIRMINGHAM CITY

WIGAN ATHLETIC

CARDIFF CITY

SHEFFIELD WEDNESDAY

PETERBOROUGH UNITED

HARTLEPOOL UNITED

IPSWICH TOWN

QUEENS PARK RANGERS

PORTSMOUTH

READING

AFC WIMBLEDON

WEST BROMWICH ALBION

ROCHDALE

GILLINGHAM

BARROW

BOURNEMOUTH

COLCHESTER UNITED

HULL CITY

LUTON TOWN

BLACKPOOL

CARLISLE UNITED

COVENTRY CITY

MANCHESTER CITY

WYCOMBE WANDERERS

STOCKPORT COUNTY

-MASCOTS-

Every professional club in the UK has a mascot, a character that represents the team. Mascots can be an animal, a human or anything at all and are supposed to bring the club good luck.

BEHIND THE MASCOT

Clubs employ people to wear giant mascot costumes for games. Their role is to cheer on the team and create a fun atmosphere. We spoke to Diane Winnard, who performs as Crusty the Pie, the Wigan mascot.

Are you the only person who is Crusty?

No, three of us take it in turns to bring Crusty to life.

Why is the mascot called Crusty?

In 2019, the club ran a competition for local children to design a new club mascot. Everyone in Wigan loves pies and Crusty was the winner!

How long do you stay in the costume for?

The costume is extremely hot and, after a period of time, quite heavy! The maximum time is one hour, though on hotter days, this is reduced to 30 minutes.

What do you do on a match-day?

Crusty arrives three hours before kick-off and greets the children who are our match-day mascots. The Pie then visits the hospitality lounges to meet the guests, before heading outside to welcome all our supporters to the stadium.

Are you good at football?

Absolutely not! It's difficult to run inside the costume as the feet are so big. But I'm great at dancing, cheering and jumping to get the crowds motivated.

Gully the Seagull
(Brighton & Hove Albion)

Frogmore the Frog
(Portsmouth)

-THE ENGLISH LEAGUE-
PYRAMID

The league system in England and Wales is structured as a pyramid of leagues. Teams move between tiers, through promotion or relegation, to the various leagues.

Professional

Semi-professional

Amateur

Women's Super League

Women's Championship

Northern Premier Division

Southern Premier Division

Division One North

Division One Midlands

Division One South West

Division One South East

8 regional leagues

17 regional leagues

34 regional leagues

WOMEN'S FOOTBALL LEAGUE

This pyramid shows the top seven tiers of English women's football. The highest tier is the Women's Super League (WSL), which was founded in 2011 and went professional in 2018. (The first time the FA organized a national league for women was in 1991.) At the moment, the top two tiers have 12 teams in them, though each league is expected to grow in the coming years.

Every team in one of these seven tiers is allowed to compete in the FA Cup. The WSL teams enter the FA Cup in the fourth round, as the tournament reaches the last 32. This means that WSL teams only need five successive wins to take the trophy.

Premier League

Championship

League One

League Two

National League

National League North   National League South

Northern Premier   Southern Central   Isthmian   Southern South

Lower divisions of the Northern Premier, Southern and Isthmian Leagues

16 regional leagues

17 regional leagues

MEN'S FOOTBALL LEAGUE

This pyramid shows the first ten tiers of English men's football. The summit is the Premier League, which has twenty teams, with three being relegated every year. Every team competing in one of these ten tiers is allowed to compete in the FA Cup. The best FA Cup run for a team outside the top four tiers came in 2017 when Lincoln City, then in the National League, reached the quarter finals.

The Isthmian League covers London and the South East. (The name is from ancient Greek, and was adopted by the league more than a hundred years ago when referencing the classical world in sport was fashionable.)

Below the top ten tiers are as many as ten more tiers consisting of hundreds more leagues and thousands of teams. The structure of these leagues varies from year to year.

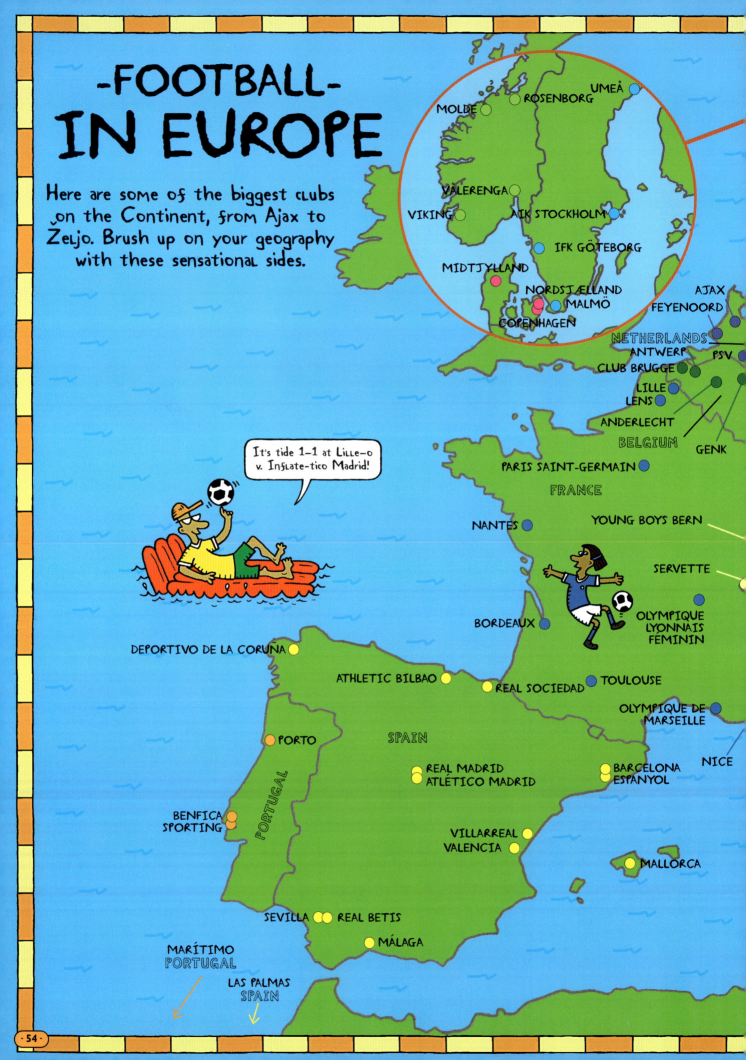

-FOOTBALL-
IN EUROPE

Here are some of the biggest clubs on the Continent, from Ajax to Željo. Brush up on your geography with these sensational sides.

MOLDE
ROSENBORG
UMEÅ
VÅLERENGA
VIKING
AIK STOCKHOLM
IFK GÖTEBORG
MIDTJYLLAND
NORDSJÆLLAND
MALMÖ
COPENHAGEN

AJAX
FEYENOORD
NETHERLANDS
ANTWERP
PSV
CLUB BRUGGE
LILLE
LENS
ANDERLECHT
BELGIUM
GENK

It's tide 1–1 at Lille–o v. Inflate–tico Madrid!

PARIS SAINT-GERMAIN
FRANCE

YOUNG BOYS BERN

NANTES

SERVETTE

OLYMPIQUE
LYONNAIS
FEMININ

BORDEAUX

DEPORTIVO DE LA CORUÑA

ATHLETIC BILBAO
REAL SOCIEDAD
TOULOUSE

OLYMPIQUE DE
MARSEILLE

PORTO
SPAIN
NICE

REAL MADRID
ATLÉTICO MADRID
BARCELONA
ESPANYOL

PORTUGAL

BENFICA
SPORTING

VILLARREAL
VALENCIA

MALLORCA

SEVILLA   REAL BETIS

MÁLAGA

MARÍTIMO
PORTUGAL

LAS PALMAS
SPAIN

Let's zoom around Europe and discover fab facts about top clubs.

AC Milan
⚽ Founded by an Englishman, the club has a red-and-black kit that is designed to look like the devil.
⚽ AC stands for *Associazione Calcio*, meaning "football association" in Italian.

Ajax
⚽ Netherlands' most successful club.
⚽ Famous youth system established by former player Johan Cruyff, in whose honour they retired the No. 14 shirt.

Anderlecht
⚽ Belgium's most successful club.
⚽ Full name is Royal Sporting Club Anderlecht; their kit is purple to match the colour of the Belgian monarchy.

Athletic Bilbao
⚽ Spain's third most successful club; they have never been relegated – impressive as they only select players from the local Basque region.

Atlético Madrid
⚽ Nicknamed The Colchoneros (Mattress-Makers in Spanish), as their red-and-white striped kit is the same colour as old-fashioned mattresses.

Barcelona
⚽ Signed Lionel Messi aged thirteen in 2001, then won ten Spanish league titles with him.
⚽ La Masia youth academy graduates include Pedri, Gavi and Ansu Fati.

Bayern Munich
⚽ Germany's richest and most successful club, they won all six trophies available in 2020, and in 2022, clinched their tenth title in a row.

Benfica
⚽ Portugal's most successful club.
⚽ Real-life eagle mascot, called Vitória, flies round their stadium in Lisbon before every home match.

Borussia Dortmund
⚽ Famous for their noisy fans; their stadium in western Germany has the Yellow Wall, a stand for 25,000 fans behind one goal.

Club Brugge
⚽ Only Belgian side to reach a European Cup final, which they lost, in 1978.
⚽ Mascot is three bears, the symbol of the Belgian city.

Dinamo Zagreb
⚽ Croatia's most successful club; famous for its excellent youth academy, which produced Luka Modrić and Mateo Kovačić.

Nordsjælland
⚽ Danish club with a focus on player education.
⚽ Same owners run Ghana's Right to Dream academy, so young players do exchange trips between the two.

Fenerbahçe
⚽ Nicknamed The Yellow Canaries, they have never been relegated from Turkey's top league.
⚽ Famous players include Roberto Carlos and Mesut Özil.

Ferencváros
⚽ Hungary's most successful side in Europe.
⚽ The Green Eagles were the first team from Hungary to play in the Champions League group stage in 1995.

FFC Frankfurt
⚽ German women's team has won the Champions League four times, the second most in history, most recently in 2015.

Galatasaray
⚽ Turkey's most successful club, and the first Turkish club to win a European trophy, the UEFA Cup, in 2000.

Grasshopper Zürich
⚽ Switzerland's most successful club.
⚽ Founded by an Englishman in 1886 who brought them a Blackburn Rovers shirt, hence their blue-and-white halves kit.

Internazionale
⚽ Based in Milan, first Italian side to win the European Cup, in 1964.
⚽ Have been in Italy's top division since 1929, longer than anyone else.

Juventus
⚽ Italy's most successful club, named after the Italian word for "youth".
⚽ Owned by the Agnelli family, who also own the Fiat car company.

Legia Warsaw
- ⚽ Poland's most successful club.
- ⚽ Passionate atmosphere where fans regularly unfurl giant banners and throw flares to show support.

Malmö
- ⚽ Sweden's most successful club and the only Scandinavian side to reach a European Cup final, in 1979.
- ⚽ Where striker Zlatan Ibrahimović began his career.

Maribor
- ⚽ Slovenia's most successful club, and the only one from the country to reach the Champions League group stage.
- ⚽ Play in purple; nicknamed The Violets.

Nantes
- ⚽ Has its own style, *le jeu à la nantaise*; promoted collective movement.
- ⚽ Academy developed France's World Cup-winning player and coach Didier Deschamps.

Olympiacos
- ⚽ Greece's most successful club, and the first Greek club to win five titles or more in a row on five separate occasions.

Olympique de Marseille
- ⚽ First French club to win the Champions League in 1993.
- ⚽ Called Olympique in honour of Greeks who founded the city in 600 BC.

Olympique Lyonnais Féminin
- ⚽ French club has won eight women's Champions League titles, more than anyone else, including five in a row between 2016 and 2020.

Paris Saint-Germain
- ⚽ One of world's richest clubs, owned by a fund from Qatar.
- ⚽ Paid world record fee of €222m for Neymar – then signed Mbappé and Messi!

Porto
- ⚽ Based in the north of Portugal, they play in blue and white, the colours of Portugal's original flag until 1910.

Rapid Vienna
- ⚽ Austria's most successful club, though their last title win was in 2008.
- ⚽ During WWII, they played in the German league and won it in 1941.

Real Madrid
- ⚽ Europe's most successful club. Won Champions League and Spanish league most often.
- ⚽ Eight different Ballon d'Or winners, including Ronaldo and Benzema.

Red Bull Salzburg
- ⚽ Previously known as Austria Salzburg until Red Bull took over in 2005.
- ⚽ Brilliant at spotting talent, helping the careers of players like Mané and Haaland.

Red Star Belgrade
- ⚽ Also known as Crvena Zvezda – "Red Star" in Serbian.
- ⚽ Only the second Eastern European team to win the European Cup, in 1991.

Roma
- ⚽ Based in the Italian capital, Roma's badge shows a mythical she-wolf suckling Rome's city founders, Romulus and Remus.

Rosenborg
- ⚽ Based in Trondheim, the food capital of Norway.
- ⚽ Norway's most successful club, having won thirteen consecutive titles between 1992 and 2004.

Slovan Bratislava
- ⚽ Slovakia's most successful club; won four titles in a row from 2019.
- ⚽ Supplied majority of players to Czechoslovakia's winning 1976 Euros team.

Sparta Prague
- ⚽ Czech Republic's most successful club.
- ⚽ Rivalry with Prague neighbour Slavia began in 1896 when a referee disallowed a Sparta winner.

St Pauli
- ⚽ Known for their German fans' rebellious spirit, support of social issues and welcoming of outsiders.
- ⚽ Fan symbol is a skull and crossbones.

Steaua Bucharest
- ⚽ Romania's most successful club, the first Eastern European winner of the European Cup, beating Barcelona 4–0 on penalties in 1986.

Umeå
- ⚽ Swedish women's club which won two and lost three Champions League finals in the 2000s.
- ⚽ First European club to sign Brazil superstar Marta.

-EURO COMPETITIONS-
CHAMPIONS LEAGUE

In 1955, UEFA set up the European Cup, a competition between every country's league champions to determine the best team in the continent. It expanded in 1992 into the Champions League.

WINNERS' WHEEL

This wheel shows the winners, and the year of success, of every European Cup and Champions League competition up to 2022.

EIGHT FABULOUS FINALS

Here are the most memorable European Cup and Champions League finals.

FIVE IN A ROW
Real Madrid 7 Eintracht Frankfurt 3

A crowd of over 130,000 fans at Glasgow's Hampden Park watched the highest-scoring final in history. Madrid striker Alfredo Di Stéfano scored a hat-trick and team-mate Ferenc Puskás four goals (he remains the only player to have ever scored four in a final) as Real Madrid won the final for the fifth time in a row. This victory established their status as Europe's premier club.

1960

HAIL LISBON LIONS
Celtic 2 Internazionale 1

Celtic became the first British side to win the European Cup with a team that were almost all born within 10 miles of their home stadium. The final took place in Portugal's capital, and the team became known as The Lisbon Lions.

1967

1968

UNITED REDEMPTION
Manchester United 4 Benfica 1

Inspired by England's World Cup-winner Bobby Charlton, Manchester United won the European Cup for the first time, ten years after eight United players died in the Munich Air Disaster in 1958. The success cemented United's place as one of England's most-loved teams.

A FOREST FIRST
Nottingham Forest 1 Malmö 0

Nottingham Forest won the European Cup at their first attempt, having won the English league in their first season after promotion. Coach Brian Clough was the mastermind. Forest repeated their European success the following season, beating Hamburg 1–0 in the final.

1979

MILAN MASTERCLASS
AC Milan 4 Steaua Bucharest 0

Milan coach Arrigo Sacchi ended Italian football's defensive reputation with a high-pressing team nicknamed The Immortals. Sacchi's bold attacking approach featured Carlo Ancelotti in midfield and Dutch superstars Ruud Gullit and Marco van Basten up front, and inspired the methods of modern coaches Pep Guardiola and Jürgen Klopp.

1989

MIRACLE OF ISTANBUL
AC Milan 3 Liverpool 3
(Liverpool win 4–2 on penalties)

Turkey's largest city hosted one of the most dramatic finals in history. Liverpool were 3–0 down at half-time, but three quick goals in the second half forced a penalty shoot-out, which they won 4–2. Miraculous!

BALE OFF THE BENCH
Real Madrid 3 Liverpool 1

Another historic achievement for Real Madrid, as they became the first team to win three Champions League titles in a row. It only happened thanks to Welsh super-sub Gareth Bale, whose first touch was a stunning overhead kick to put the Spaniards ahead. Bale then scored another with a shot from 40 yards out.

2005

TUCHEL TURNAROUND
Chelsea 1 Manchester City 0

Chelsea claimed their second Champions League title after an all-English final, only six months after appointing Thomas Tuchel as their new coach. Tuchel turned the team's fortunes around, as his fellow German Kai Havertz scored the winning goal on the counter-attack.

2018

2021

WOMEN'S CHAMPIONS LEAGUE

In 2002, 33 clubs entered the first European competition for female players, originally called the UEFA Women's Cup. The 2022 version had 72 teams from 50 different countries.

WINNERS' WHEEL

This image shows the winners, and the year of success, of every UEFA Women's Cup and Women's Champions League competition up to 2022.

Olympique Lyonnais Féminin
2022
2020
2019
2018
2017
2016
2012
2011
8

FFC Frankfurt
2015
2008
2006
2002
4

Duisburg
2009
1

Arsenal
2007
1

Barcelona
2021
1

2005
2

Turbine Potsdam
2010

2013
2014
VFL Wolfsburg
2

Umeå
2004
2003
2

PERFECT PAIR

Here are two of the most dramatic women's European finals.

SCOTT STUNS SWEDES
Arsenal 1 Umeå 0

Swedish side Umeå won the competition, then called the UEFA Women's Cup, in 2003 and 2004. With Brazilian superstar Marta in their line-up, they were favourites to beat Arsenal. Alex Scott scored a long-distance winner in the last minute of the first leg and Arsenal held on to become the first British women's team to win in Europe.

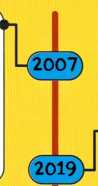

2007

2019

HEROIC HEGERBERG
Olympique Lyonnais Féminin 4 Barcelona 1

Olympique Lyonnais Féminin won eight out of twelve European titles starting in 2010. The highlight? In 2019, they humbled Barcelona 4–1, thanks to a sixteen-minute hat-trick from Ada Hegerberg, the competition's all-time leading goal-scorer. Hegerberg also scored in Lyon's 3–1 final win against the same opposition in the 2022 final.

CLUB WORLD CUP

The Club World Cup is the knockout competition between the winners of the Champions League and the five other continental competitions. It first took place in 2000 and has been held annually since 2005.

WINNERS' WHEEL

This image shows the winners, and the year of success, of every Club World Cup up to 2022.

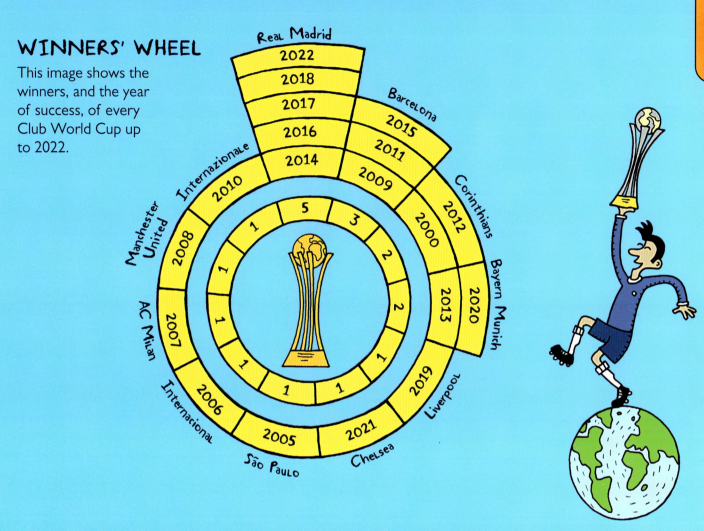

OTHER CONTINENTAL CLUB COMPETITIONS

Every continent has a knockout competition for their best clubs.

OCEANIA CHAMPIONS LEAGUE
First final: 1987
Most wins: Auckland City (New Zealand), 9

NORTH AMERICA CHAMPIONS LEAGUE
First final: 1962
Most wins: Club América (Mexico), 7

ASIA CHAMPIONS LEAGUE
First final: 1967
Most wins: Al Hilal (Saudi Arabia), 4

AFRICA CHAMPIONS LEAGUE
First final: 1965
Most wins: Al Ahly (Egypt), 10

SOUTH AMERICA COPA LIBERTADORES
First final: 1960
Most wins: Independiente (Argentina), 7

-FOOTBALL ACROSS THE WORLD-

Here's a selection of the biggest clubs from the Americas, Africa, Asia and Australia. It's the global football A-list!

CANADA

JS KABYLIE
ALGERIA

ESPÉRANCE DE TUNIS
TUNISIA

OL REIGN

PORTLAND THORNS

TORONTO

USA

WYDAD
MOROCCO

REAL SALT LAKE

COLUMBUS CREW
DC UNITED

NEW YORK RED BULLS

STADE MALIEN
MALI

LA GALAXY

ATLANTA UNITED

MEXICO

GUADALAJARA
CLUB AMÉRICA
CRUZ AZUL

ASANTE KOTOKO
GHANA

We're Goal-ápagos penguins!

ATLÉTICO NACIONAL
MILLONARIOS

COLOMBIA

BARCELONA
ECUADOR

FLAMENGO
FLUMINENSE
PALMEIRAS
SÃO PAULO
CORINTHIANS
SANTOS

UNIVERSITARIO
PERU

BAHIA

BRAZIL

BOLÍVAR
BOLIVIA

CRUZEIRO

OLIMPIA
PARAGUAY

GRÊMIO

COLO-COLO
CHILE

RIVER
PLATE

PEÑAROL
NACIONAL

BOCA JUNIORS

NEWELL'S OLD BOYS

URUGUAY

INDEPENDIENTE

ARGENTINA

Most of Russia is in Asia, even if its big teams are in Europe.

N
W
E
S

ZENIT
URAL
CSKA MOSCOW SPARTAK MOSCOW
RUSSIA

ASTANA
KAZAKHSTAN

POHANG STEELERS
SOUTH KOREA

YOKOHAMA MARINOS
KAWASAKI FRONTALE
KOBE LEONESSA
JAPAN

PERSEPOLIS
IRAN
SHANDONG TAISHAN
CHINA

AL AHLY
ZAMALEK
EGYPT
MACCABI TEL AVIV
ISRAEL

AL HILAL
SAUDI ARABIA
AL AIN
UAE
GUANGZHOU

ELECT-SPORT
CHAD

BURIRAM UNITED
THAILAND

ENYIMBA
NIGERIA

COTON SPORT
CAMEROON

TP MAZEMBE
DEMOCRATIC
REPUBLIC OF
CONGO

PETRÓLEOS
DE LUANDA
ANGOLA

AUSTRALIA

BRISBANE ROAR

MAMELODI SUNDOWNS
KAIZER CHIEFS
SOUTH AFRICA

SYDNEY

MELBOURNE VICTORY

WELLINGTON PHOENIX
NEW ZEALAND

Discover wonderful facts about the biggest world clubs.

Al Ahly
- Based in Cairo, Egypt, they have won the most trophies in world football.
- Most successful team in the Africa Champions League, with ten titles.

Al Hilal
- Based in Riyadh, Saudi Arabia, they won their fourth Asia Champions League in 2021, the first team to do so.

Asante Kotoko
- The club – known as The Porcupine Warriors – are the most successful in Ghana, and won the Africa Champions League in 1970 and 1983.

Atlanta United
- Set up in 2017, the USA team won the Major League Soccer Cup in 2018.
- Hold the record for largest attendance in the league.

Atlético Nacional
- The most successful Colombian club in the Copa Libertadores, with two titles.
- Their nickname, The Verdolagas, means "purslane", a green herb.

Boca Juniors
- The Buenos Aires club are the most supported in Argentina.
- They won the continental trophy, the Copa Libertadores, for the sixth time in 2007.

Bolívar
- Named after the South American freedom fighter Simon Bolívar, the La Paz club are Bolivia's most successful side.

Club América
- Known as The Eagles, they are based in Mexico City and have won more trophies than any other Mexican team.

Colo-Colo
- The biggest and most successful club in Chile.
- Named after an Indigenous leader who fought against the Spanish colonizers in the sixteenth century.

Columbus Crew
- USA club and world-record holders for the longest chain of scarves held by fans, measuring over one mile, to support children's mental health.

Corinthians
- The biggest club in São Paulo, Brazil's biggest city, they are double world champions, winning FIFA's Club World Cup in 2000 and 2012.

Espérance de Tunis
- Tunisia's most successful club.
- Nicknamed Blood and Gold for their red and yellow shirts, they have won the Africa Champions League four times.

Flamengo
- The Rio de Janeiro side is the most supported club in Brazil, with a distinctive kit of black-and-red horizontal stripes.

Fluminense
- Four-time Brazilian champions, most recently in 2012.
- Their Rio de Janeiro stadium hosted the first match of the national team in 1914.

Grêmio
- Founded by the German community in Porto Alegre, Brazil, they have won the Copa Libertadores three times.

Guadalajara
- Known by their nickname Chivas, meaning goats, the club has picked only Mexican players since 1908.

Guangzhou
- The most successful club in China, and the only one to have won the Asia Champions League twice, in 2013 and 2015.

JS Kabylie
- From Kabylie, a Berber region of Algeria, they are the country's most successful club, with two Africa Champions League titles: 1981 and 1990.

Kawasaki Frontale
- Based in Kawasaki, part of Tokyo, they won four Japanese league titles between 2017 and 2021.
- The name Frontale means "in the front".

Kobe Leonessa
- ⚽ Winners in 2022 of the first season of the WE League, the first professional women's league in Japan.

LA Galaxy
- ⚽ Most successful team in Major League Soccer. David Beckham and Steven Gerrard played for the USA club at the end of their careers.

Mamelodi Sundowns
- ⚽ Based in Pretoria, they are the most successful South African club of this century, winning seven league titles between 2013 and 2022.

Nacional
- ⚽ Uruguayan team from Montevideo that has won the Copa Libertadores three times.
- ⚽ Their passionate fans once made a flag 600m long – a world record!

Newell's Old Boys
- ⚽ Argentinian club from Rosario, famous for its youth academy.
- ⚽ Many top players emerged here, including Lionel Messi and Mauricio Pochettino.

Olimpia
- ⚽ Based in the Paraguayan capital, Asunción.
- ⚽ They are the only Paraguayan club to have won the Copa Libertadores, in 1979, 1990 and 2002.

OL Reign
- ⚽ Formerly Seattle Reign, the USA women's club changed their name in 2020 when bought by the company that owns Olympique Lyonnais Féminin.

Palmeiras
- ⚽ Founded by São Paulo's Italian community, they currently have the record for the most Brazilian league titles.

Peñarol
- ⚽ Based in the Uruguayan capital Montevideo, they are five-time winners of the Copa Libertadores, and the first club of striker Darwin Núñez.

Persepolis
- ⚽ Iran's most successful team.
- ⚽ They have the Asia Champions League attendance record: 100,000 fans at their stadium in Tehran.

Pohang Steelers
- ⚽ Formed by a steel company in Pohang, South Korea, they are one of the strongest Asian teams, with three Champions League titles.

Portland Thorns
- ⚽ Founded in 2012, they have the highest attendance in the USA women's league.
- ⚽ Canadian striker Christine Sinclair is their all-time top scorer.

River Plate
- ⚽ Argentina's most successful club in domestic competitions.
- ⚽ They play at the Monumental, in Buenos Aires, the biggest stadium in the country.

Santos
- ⚽ From the coastal city of Santos, where Brazil legends Pelé and Neymar began their careers.
- ⚽ Nicknamed Peixe – meaning "fish".

São Paulo
- ⚽ The only Brazilian club with three world titles: the Intercontinental Cup in 1992 and 1993, and the Club World Cup in 2005.

Sydney
- ⚽ The most successful team in Australia. Because the country is part of the Asian confederation, the club play regularly in the Asia Champions League.

Toronto
- ⚽ Along with Vancouver Whitecaps, the Reds are one of two Canadian teams to play Major League Soccer in the USA.

Universitario
- ⚽ Founded by students and professors at a Lima university, they were the first Peruvian team to reach a Copa Libertadores final, in 1972.

Wellington Phoenix
- ⚽ The club are the only one based in New Zealand to play in the A-League, the top tier of Australian football.

Zamalek
- ⚽ The Egyptian club are the second most successful in the Africa Champions League, with five titles, behind only their local rivals Al Ahly.

-STADIUMS-

The stadiums of the world's great clubs are giant landmarks that reflect those clubs' history, culture and ambitions. Here are some of the most famous — and most curious — footballing cathedrals.

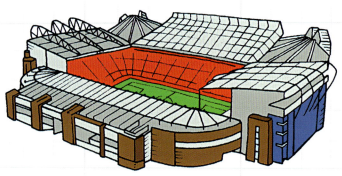

OLD TRAFFORD

Manchester United's stadium was built in 1910 with an original capacity of 80,000. Bombed during the Second World War, it was then rebuilt. Only the central players' tunnel remains from the original structure. In the 1980s, club legend Bobby Charlton called it the Theatre of Dreams, which has stuck. With a capacity of 74,140, it is the biggest club stadium in the UK.

TOTTENHAM HOTSPUR STADIUM

Built in 2019, with a capacity of 62,850, the stadium is London's biggest and has many innovations. The grass football pitch splits into three parts and can be rolled away to leave a pitch of artificial turf underneath, used for American football. The stadium has special acoustic panels in the roof to make fans' cheers as loud as possible.

WESTFALENSTADION

For years Borussia Dortmund's stadium — Germany's largest, with a capacity of 81,365 — has been Europe's best-attended football ground, averaging more than 80,000 every game. It is known for its amazing atmosphere, particularly in the south terrace, which fits almost 25,000 people and is the largest standing area in a European stadium.

CAMP NOU

Camp Nou — meaning "new field" — has been a stadium of superlatives since 1954, when 60,000 fans showed up to watch the first stone being laid. It is the biggest club stadium in Europe by far, with a capacity of 99,354, almost 20,000 larger than the next biggest. It is a symbol of Barcelona's ambition to be the greatest club in the world.

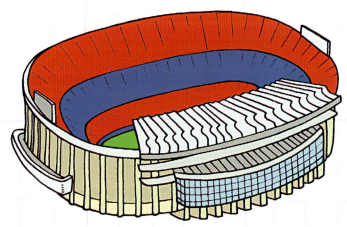

I am Archibald Leitch, football's most famous architect. Between 1899 and 1939 I designed more than twenty stadiums in the UK, including Old Trafford, Anfield, Stamford Bridge, Craven Cottage, Ibrox and Celtic Park. Archi-bald by name, Archi-tect, by nature!

LA BOMBONERA

Boca Juniors' stadium is one of the most legendary in South America. Argentina's most popular side built it in 1940 in the port area of Buenos Aires, where there wasn't much available land. The stands are very close to the pitch, high and very steep (La Bombonera means "chocolate box"). When its 57,000 fans get chanting, the atmosphere is electric.

TIMSAH ARENA

When Bursaspor – known as The Green Crocodiles – won their first-ever Turkish league title in 2010, the club decided to build a 43,000-capacity stadium in the shape of … a crocodile! They are now desperate to have another bite at the trophy!

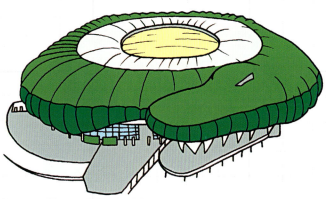

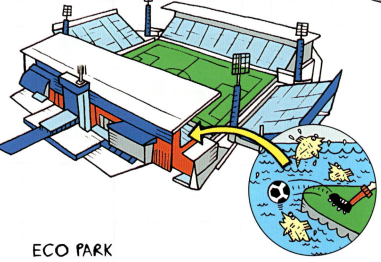

MAPEI STADIUM

If you tire of watching football at the home ground of Italian Serie A side Sassuolo, you can always pass the time fishing. The stadium has a moat between the stands and the pitch. Water from a nearby river flows into the moat, bringing fish with it. At Mapei, the catch of the day is not always made by the goalkeeper, but by a fan with a fishing rod!

ECO PARK

In 2019, English club Forest Green Rovers were given planning permission to build a 5,000-seater football stadium made almost entirely from wood. It will be the world's greenest stadium and also involve the club planting 500 trees and 1.8 km of hedges.

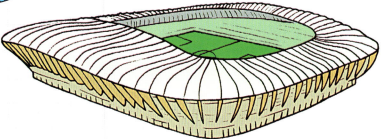

-THE STRUCTURE OF-
A FOOTBALL CLUB

A professional club is a business with an organizational structure that may look like this one. On the opposite page is how the club makes money and spends it.

OWNER
Buys the club and appoints key personnel to run it. They can make any big decision.

DIRECTORS
Plan and make decisions for the club's long-term success.

CHIEF EXECUTIVE OFFICER
In charge of the everyday running of the club and responsible for all the departments.

HUMAN RESOURCES
Looks after all employees, making sure everyone who works in the club is happy and engaged.

FINANCE
Makes sure the club is spending what it can afford.

FOOTBALL OPERATIONS
Oversees all sporting areas and makes sure all departments are pulling in the same direction — towards success!

MARKETING
Presents a positive image of the club to the public and brings in money through sponsors and other partnerships.

EVENTS
Uses stadium and club facilities to organize and host other events, including concerts, conferences or other sports.

MEMBERSHIP
Develops and grows a loyal fan-base who bring money into the club.

HEAD COACH
Trains and selects the first team; usually has a contract of two or three years.

BACKROOM STAFF
Support the coach to improve the players' tactics, technique and fitness.

PLAYERS
A squad of up to 25 professionals who play for the first team.

RECRUITMENT
Selects and buys players to improve the first team. Sells players to raise funds.

ACADEMY
Develops young players capable of moving up to play for the first team.

MEDICAL
Prevents injuries with specialist training and helps injured players recover quickly.

MONEY MATTERS

Like all businesses, clubs have money coming in, called revenue, and money going out, called expenditure. Here we look at how the money breaks down at an average Premier League club.

REVENUE

The revenue is the money that each club receives from the following sources:

Premier League fees: **60%**
TV companies give the Premier League billions of pounds for the rights to show matches. The league then distributes this money to every club in the following way:
- £80m fixed fee
- £1.9m per place they finish in the table (the top club gets £38m)
- £1.1m each time their match is on TV
- A share of foreign TV rights

Sponsors' fees: **27%**
This comes from sponsors whose names appear on the kit and around the stadium.

Match-day earnings: **13%**
The money made from fans buying tickets, eating food and buying merchandise.

TOTAL REVENUE   **100%**

EXPENDITURE

The expenditure is the money that each club spends on the following resources:

Player salaries: **57%**
Paying wages to players is the biggest cost to clubs.

Player trading: **26%**
The money paid in transfer fees for new players minus the money made from selling players. For big clubs, trading players is always expenditure not revenue.

Other fees: **12%**
This includes insurance costs, medical bills and stadium upkeep.

Agents' fees: **5%**
The money clubs pay to agents to help them sign players they want.

TOTAL EXPENDITURE   **100%**

-INSIDE THE WORLD OF-
TRANSFERS

Football transfers happen when a club organizes for a player to move from one club to another. Signing the right players can transform the fortunes of a club – but getting the wrong ones can have the opposite effect!

TRANSFER TYPES

When big players are on the move, it can mean clubs are spending huge amounts of money. However, most transfers are for little or no money. There are four types of transfer:

1. **Out of contract:** When the player has come to the end of their contract.
2. **Loan:** When the player joins another team for a short period, sometimes for a small fee.
3. **Permanent:** When the player joins another team for a fee.
4. **Return from loan:** When the player returns from their short period away.

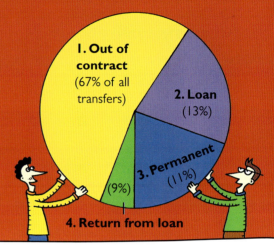

1. Out of contract (67% of all transfers)
2. Loan (13%)
3. Permanent (11%)
(9%)
4. Return from loan

TRANSFER GLOSSARY

Let's learn about transfers!

Get a move on, then!

The world of transfers contains many words that you only hear when players are moving clubs. Here are some useful terms to know.

Agent: Also known as an intermediary, this is an advisor to a player who helps negotiate contracts with clubs.

Amortization: The way a club spreads the transfer fee over the length of a player's contract. A £50m player on a five-year contract does not mean £50m spent in one go, but, say, £10m per year for the next five years.

Contract: A legal document that ties a player to a club.

Free agent: A player who is out of contract. If a player allows their contract to expire, the buying club do not have to pay a transfer fee.

Medical: A player about to sign for a new club has a full medical check to ensure the club are not spending lots of money on someone who is injured.

Release clause: A line in the contract that allows the player to leave if a certain amount is offered.

TMS (Transfer Matching System): The system all clubs use to process and complete a transfer. The system is run by FIFA, which releases an International Transfer Certificate to complete the player's registration.

Transfer window: The period during which transfers can happen. It is usually during the summer (between seasons) and for one month in January.

Value: The value of a player, which is how much a club are willing to pay, can depend on many factors, including length of remaining contract, age, salary, position and even nationality.

THE STORY OF A PERMANENT TRANSFER

The most expensive transfers are permanent transfers, and they receive the most attention and media coverage. Let's look at how a big transfer works.

Player X is in top form for Club A, where he is under contract for three years. Club B wants to sign him.

Club B calls Club A requesting permission to ask if Player X wants to move. Player X is keen.

Club B negotiates a transfer fee with Club A to buy Player X.

Club B agrees and signs a Transfer Contract with Club A and a Player Contract with Player X.

Player X takes a medical at Club B.

Club B inputs all the transfer details into the FIFA TMS database. Player X can now play for Club B!

-THE CLUBS- QUIZ

1. Here are some facts about clubs in the UK and Europe. Match the fact to the club.

1) Play in purple   a) Anderlecht
2) Were bought for £2.5 billion   b) St Pauli
3) Fans' symbol is a pirate flag   c) Lewes
4) First gender-equal club   d) Chelsea

2. Which is the only team in the English football league to wear red-and-black stripes?

a) Bournemouth
b) Gillingham
c) Bradford City
d) Crystal Palace

3. Which naughty mascot forced football bosses to write strict rules for club mascots?

a) Swansea's Cyril the Swan
b) Arsenal's Gunnersaurus
c) Bury's Robbie the Bobby
d) Brighton's Gully the Seagull

4. How did Ferenc Puskás make European Cup final history in the 1960 final, the match in which Real Madrid won the trophy for a fifth consecutive time?

a) He is the only player to score four goals.
b) He is the only player to set up seven goals.
c) He is the only player to play in five consecutive finals and win them all.
d) All of the above.

5. Which of the following English teams has won the European Cup or Champions League just once?

a) Chelsea
b) Nottingham Forest
c) Aston Villa
d) Manchester United

6. Which team has won the women's Champions League the second-most times, behind Olympique Lyonnais Féminin?

a) Duisburg
b) UFL Wolfsburg
c) FFC Frankfurt
d) Bayern Munich

7. These clubs have won their major continental tournament the most times. Match the club to the country where they play.

1) Real Madrid   a) Argentina
2) Independiente   b) New Zealand
3) Al Ahly   c) Egypt
4) Auckland City   d) Mexico
5) Al Hilal   e) Spain
6) Club América   f) Saudi Arabia

8. What do the stadiums belonging to Manchester United, Liverpool, Chelsea, Fulham and Celtic all have in common?

a) They all have a retractable roof.
b) Each has a train station named after it.
c) When each one was built, it was the biggest stadium in the UK at the time.
d) They used the same original architect.

9. What do the majority of football clubs spend most of their money on?

a) Looking after the stadium
b) Player salaries
c) Transfer fees
d) Insurance costs

10. What is a free agent?

a) Someone who helps players find a new club and doesn't charge a fee
b) A player who can play in any position
c) A player who works for free
d) A player who is out of contract

Answers: 1. 1) a, 2) d, 3) b, 4) c, 2. a, 3. c, 4. a, 5. c, 6. c, 7. 1) e, 2) a, 3) c, 4) b, 5) f, 6) d, 8. d, 9. b, 10. d

3. THE COUNTRIES

National teams, national styles and the most prestigious tournament of all: the World Cup!

-THE BIRTH OF-
INTERNATIONAL FOOTBALL

The first football match between nations was Scotland v. England in 1872. Within decades, many other countries had their own national teams.

THE F⚽⚽TBALL TIMES

Goalless in Glasgow

SPECIAL EDITION

Scotland and England drew 0–0 on November 30, 1872, in what is considered the first-ever football international. About 4,000 people watched the match, which took place at the West of Scotland Cricket Club's ground in Glasgow.

The idea for an international game had originated with the FA, who wanted to promote football across the UK. In 1870, the FA had placed adverts in Scottish newspapers calling for Scots to play a game that year in London against English players.

In the end the Scottish team were made up almost entirely of London-based players claiming Scottish heritage. The first game in which the Scotland team were actually made up of Scots playing in Scotland was the 1872 game in Glasgow.

In 1876, Wales established its own national team and in 1882, Ireland did too. In 1884, the four home nations established the British Home Championship, the oldest international tournament in the world, which ran until 1984. Home run!

All aboard!

Football in South America: on track

The British introduced football to countries all over the world, but no continent embraced the game as early, or as enthusiastically, as South America. And it largely happened because of steam trains. We kid choo-choo not!

Many Brits moved to South America in the second half of the 19th century to build railways. They took footballs with them. In 1867, the British community in Argentina, mostly made up of railway workers, founded the first football club outside the UK.

It was a similar story in Brazil, where Charles Miller, the Brazilian-born son of a Scottish railway worker, helped set up the country's first league in 1902.

Uruguay emerged as the strongest team in the continent. In 1916, they won the first South American Football Championship (now called the Copa América). They also won gold at both the 1924 and the 1928 Olympics, and hosted and won the first World Cup in 1930. Yoo-hoo for Uruguay!

Game changers

Isabelino Gradín

Uruguay was the first country in the world to field Black players in its national team. Isabelino Gradín (1897–1944) was only 19 when he was top scorer in Uruguay's victory in the 1916 South American Football Championship. José Leandro Andrade (1901–57) was a key player in the side's two Olympic and one World Cup titles.

José Leandro Andrade

LE MONDE F⚽⚽TBALL

ÉDITION SPÉCIALE

Les nations s'unissent*

In Paris in 1904, seven countries – France, Belgium, Spain, Denmark, the Netherlands, Sweden and Switzerland – founded the Fédération internationale de football association, or FIFA, the sport's global governing body. Germany joined soon after and England became a member in 1906. The birth of FIFA – which adopted the FA's Laws of the Game – was an important step in the growth of football from a British pastime to a global sport. But just as international football was expanding, the First World War (1914–18) put everything on hold.

The war, however, had unexpected consequences. In 1921, Frenchman Jules Rimet, who had served as a soldier in the French army, became FIFA president. Having witnessed the horrors of war first-hand, he was determined to use football to promote peace and co-operation between nations. He pushed the organization to stage a global professional tournament. As a result of his efforts, the World Cup was born. *Vive Jules! Vive la France!*

Jules Rimet

*French translation: Nations unite

The first 20 national teams, listed by the year they played their first match:

1872: Scotland, England	1904: Belgium, France
1876: Wales	1905: Switzerland, Netherlands, Guyana, Trinidad and Tobago
1882: Ireland	1906: Sweden, Norway
1902: Uruguay, Argentina, Hungary, Austria	1908: Denmark
1903: Bohemia (now Czech Republic)	1910: Italy, Chile

-COLOURS OF THE WORLD-

Here are the flags and national team shirts and shorts of all 211 members of FIFA, football's world governing body. Each team can enter the World Cup qualifiers.

ASIA

Afghanistan
Australia
Bahrain
Bangladesh
Bhutan
Brunei Darussalam
Cambodia
China
Chinese Taipei
Guam
Hong Kong
India
Indonesia
Iran
Iraq
Japan
Jordan
Kuwait
Kyrgyzstan
Laos
Lebanon
Macau
Malaysia
Maldives
Mongolia
Myanmar
Nepal

North Korea
Oman
Pakistan
Palestine
Philippines
Qatar
Saudi Arabia
Singapore
South Korea
Sri Lanka
Syria
Tajikistan
Thailand
Timor-Leste
Turkmenistan
United Arab Emirates
Uzbekistan
Vietnam
Yemen

AFRICA

Algeria
Angola
Benin
Botswana
Burkina Faso
Burundi
Cabo Verde
Cameroon
Central African Republic
Chad
Comoros
Congo Republic
DR Congo
Djibouti
Egypt
Equatorial Guinea
Eritrea
Eswatini
Ethiopia
Gabon
Gambia
Ghana
Guinea
Guinea-Bissau
Ivory Coast
Kenya
Lesotho

Liberia
Libya
Madagascar
Malawi
Mali
Mauritania
Mauritius
Morocco
Mozambique
Namibia
Niger
Nigeria
Rwanda
São Tomé and Príncipe
Senegal
Seychelles
Sierra Leone
Somalia
South Africa
South Sudan
Sudan
Tanzania
Togo
Tunisia
Uganda
Zambia
Zimbabwe

EUROPE

 Albania

Andorra

Armenia

Austria

Azerbaijan

Belarus

Belgium

Bosnia and Herzegovina

Bulgaria

Croatia

Cyprus

Czech Republic

Denmark

England

Estonia

Faroe Islands

Finland

France

Georgia

Germany

Gibraltar

Greece

Hungary

Iceland

Ireland

Israel

Italy

Kazakhstan

Kosovo

Latvia

Liechtenstein

Lithuania

Luxembourg

Malta

Moldova

Montenegro

Netherlands

North Macedonia

Northern Ireland

Norway

Poland

Portugal

Romania

Russia

San Marino

Scotland

Serbia

Slovakia

Slovenia

Spain

Sweden

Switzerland

Turkey

Ukraine

Wales

NORTH AMERICA

Anguilla

Antigua and Barbuda

Aruba

Bahamas

Barbados

Belize

Bermuda

British Virgin Islands

Canada

Cayman Islands

Costa Rica

Cuba

Curaçao

Dominica

Dominican Republic

El Salvador

Grenada

Guatemala

Guyana

Haiti

Honduras

Jamaica

Mexico

Montserrat

Nicaragua

Panama

Puerto Rico

St Kitts and Nevis

St Lucia

St Vincent and the Grenadines

Suriname

Trinidad and Tobago

Turks and Caicos Islands

 US Virgin Islands

USA

SOUTH AMERICA

Argentina

Bolivia

Brazil

Chile

Colombia

Ecuador

Paraguay

Peru

Uruguay

Venezuela

OCEANIA

American Samoa

Cook Islands

Fiji

New Caledonia

New Zealand

Papua New Guinea

Samoa

Solomon Islands

Tahiti

Tonga

Vanuatu

-THE WORLD CUP-
MEN'S 1930 - PRESENT

The World Cup is the most watched tournament in world sport and the most prestigious prize in football. It's every player's dream to win the World Cup! Here's what happened in all the finals, from the first tournament in 1930.

URUGUAY, FIRST WORLD CHAMPIONS
Uruguay 4 Argentina 2
Hosts: Uruguay

The teams disagree on which ball to use, so Argentina choose their ball for the first half, which they win 2–1, and Uruguay use theirs for the second half, in which they score three goals. Amaze-balls!

1930

NUMERO UNO FOR ITALY
Italy 2 Czechoslovakia 1 (after extra-time)
Hosts: Italy

Italy come from behind to score a late equalizer and extra-time winner. Reigning champions Uruguay boycott the tournament because Italy scorer Raimundo Orsi had previously played for Argentina. Grumpy-guay more like!

1934

ITALY DO IT AGAIN
Italy 4 Hungary 2
Hosts: France

Captain Giuseppe Meazza, whose shorts fell down when he scored the winning penalty in the semi-final over Brazil, guides Italy to their second success. Italy become the first team to win the World Cup without hosting it. Top travellers!

1938

URUGUAY DOUBLE MAKES BRAZIL BITTER
Uruguay 1 Brazil 0
Hosts: Brazil

After a twelve-year gap because of the Second World War, almost 200,000 fans see Brazil goalkeeper Barbosa make a mistake that loses them the game. Barbosa is never forgiven by fans. According to legend, Barbosa is given, years later, the goalposts from the stadium. He cuts them into small pieces and burns them on his barbecue. Tasty!

1950

WEST GERMANY STUD SUCCESS
West Germany 3 Hungary 2
Hosts: Switzerland

Favourites Hungary are 2–0 up after just eight minutes but West Germany, helped by longer studs provided by Adidas founder Adi Dassler, make a stunning comeback. This rain-soaked match, played in the Swiss city of Bern, becomes known as the Miracle of Bern. It is a boot-iful victory for Germany!

1954

FINALLY BRAZIL, THANKS TO PELÉ
Brazil 5 Sweden 2
Hosts: Sweden

Seventeen-year-old phenomenon Pelé inspires Brazil to their first World Cup success, scoring two goals in the final. This game set the record for the youngest (Pelé, 17) and oldest scorers (Nils Liedholm, 35) in a final. It is also the first time a World Cup hosted in Europe (Sweden) was not won by a European team. It was Pelé's party!

1958

BRAZIL, TWO IN A ROW
Brazil 3 Czechoslovakia 1
Hosts: Chile

This tournament only used four stadiums as four others were damaged in a 1960 earthquake in host country Chile. Brazil became the second team to defend their title, despite losing Pelé to injury. Tricky winger Garrincha stepped up as their star player. Garrincha the clincher!

BRAZIL ARE FIRST TO THREE TITLES
Brazil 4 Italy 1
Hosts: Mexico

Brazil coach Mário Zagallo, a former team-mate of Pelé, picks an attacking team who reward his bravery with a series of high-scoring wins. Their success in the final, capped off by captain Carlos Alberto scoring at the end of a wonderful team move, remains one of the greatest team displays ever. Welcome to *o jogo bonito* – the beautiful game!

FIRST SUCCESS FOR ARGENTINA
Argentina 2 Netherlands 1
Hosts: Argentina

In a hostile atmosphere, hosts Argentina edge out the Netherlands thanks to two goals from tournament top-scorer Mario Kempes. Super Mario!

TWO UP FOR ARGENTINA
Argentina 3 West Germany 2
Hosts: Mexico

Argentina captain Diego Maradona, scorer of two goals against England in the quarter-final, seals hero status back home after setting up the winning goal for Jorge Luis Burruchaga. Dazzling Diego!

1962

1966

1970

1974

1978

1982

1986

ENGLAND BRING IT HOME
England 4 West Germany 2 (after extra time)
Hosts: England

England's Geoff Hurst, only playing because of injury to first-choice striker Jimmy Greaves, becomes the first player to score a hat-trick in a dramatic World Cup final. England's third goal hits the crossbar and bounces on the line; some German fans still think it didn't cross the line! *Ach nein!* Oh yes!

NUMBER TWO FOR WEST GERMANY
West Germany 2 Netherlands 1
Hosts: West Germany

The Netherlands score a penalty before their opponents even touch the ball and then dominate the game. West Germany score twice against the run of play and hold on to win. This Netherlands team are one of the best teams never to win the World Cup. Dutch distress!

ITALY'S TRIPLE DELIGHT
Italy 3 West Germany 1
Hosts: Spain

Italy captain and goalkeeper Dino Zoff, aged 40, becomes the oldest player to win the World Cup. Italy miss an early penalty, but recover to leave the Germans joyless. Yes, Dino!

GERMANY'S FIRST SOLO SUCCESS
Germany 1 Argentina 0
Hosts: Italy

German defender Andreas Brehme converts a late penalty to win a closely-fought and bad-tempered match in which Argentina become the first finalists to have a player sent off (two Argentines are dismissed). Argy-bargy!

1990

BRAZIL MAKE IT FOUR
Brazil 0 Italy 0 (Brazil win 3-2 on pens)
Hosts: USA

Brazil wins the first final to be decided by a penalty shoot-out after Italy's Roberto Baggio, then the best player in the world, blasts his penalty over the crossbar. That made Italians cross!

1994

FIRST TIME FOR FRANCE
France 3 Brazil 0
Hosts: USA

Midfielder Zinédine Zidane inspires France to their first World Cup victory, with two headers in the final. The match is overshadowed by a mystery surrounding Brazil forward Ronaldo, who has a quiet game after suffering a panic attack before kick-off. A Ronaldo riddle!

1998

HIGH FIVE FOR BRAZIL
Brazil 2 Germany 0
Hosts: South Korea and Japan

Injury-hit Ronaldo hasn't played for Brazil for three years before he is selected for 2002. He top-scores in the tournament, with two goals in the final to secure a record-breaking fifth title for Brazil. Rocket Ron returns!

2002

ITALY NET NUMBER FOUR
Italy 1 France 1 (Italy win 5-3 on pens)
Hosts: Germany

Zidane, France's hero in 1998, plays his last-ever game. He scores early on from the penalty spot and is then controversially sent off for head-butting an opponent. Italy then win on penalties. Boo-hoo, Zizou!

2006

SPAIN JOIN WINNERS AT LAST
Spain 1 Netherlands 0
Hosts: South Africa

Spain, made up mainly of Barcelona players, dominate opponents with possession. They win their last four matches of the tournament 1-0 for their first World Cup. In the final, midfielder Andrés Iniesta scores a dramatic late winning goal. Spain 1 World 0!

2010

GERMANY WIN SECOND TITLE
Germany 1 Argentina 0
Hosts: Brazil

Germany hammer hosts Brazil 7-1 in the semi-finals and then edge past Argentina in a close final thanks to substitute Mario Götze's volleyed finish, leaving Lionel Messi and compatriots heartbroken. The German genius!

2014

FRANCE CROWNED CHAMPS AGAIN
France 4 Croatia 2
Hosts: Russia

Kylian Mbappé, at 19 years old, becomes the youngest player since Pelé to score in a World Cup final. The teenage forward inspires France to their second World Cup title, beating first-time finalists Croatia. King Kyl!

2018

ARGENTINA MAKE IT THREE
Argentina 3 France 3 (Arg win 4-2 on pens)
Hosts: Qatar

In one of the most exciting finals ever, Kylian Mbappé scores a hat-trick to send a dramatic game to a penalty shoot-out. Argentina goalkeeper Emi Martínez saves France's first penalty, and winning captain Lionel Messi lifts the one trophy he was missing! Martínez + Messi = magic!

2022

WOMEN'S 1991 – PRESENT

The Women's World Cup was first held in 1991. Here's what happened in all the finals.

1991 — USA WIN FIRST TITLE
USA 2 Norway 0
Hosts: China

Two goals from striker Michelle Akers seal USA's victory in the first tournament, which was contested between twelve teams and named the 1st FIFA World Championship for Women's Football for the M&M's Cup. USA lead the way!

1995 — NORWAY NEW CHAMPIONS
Norway 2 Germany 0
Hosts: Sweden

Norway midfielder Hege Riise, who wins the Golden Ball for best player and would later go on to briefly manage England, scores a brilliant solo goal to set Norway up for their first success. Riise up!

1999 — USA SEIZE SECOND CROWN
USA 0 China 0 (USA win 5–4 on pens)
Hosts: USA

USA defender Brandi Chastain scores the winning penalty in the shoot-out … with her wrong foot! She takes it left-footed to confuse the goalkeeper and when it goes in, she rips off her shirt in celebration. The iconic image is seen around the world and inspires a generation of female athletes. Bran-tastic!

2003 — FIRST TITLE FOR GERMANY
Germany 2 Sweden 1 (golden goal)
Hosts: USA

Germany come from behind to win, with Nia Künzer's winning goal ending the match in extra-time. The rule then was based on a "golden goal", which ended the match as soon as one goal was scored in extra-time (the rule has now been scrapped). Künzer's header was the last-ever golden goal in an international tournament. Goal-den glory!

2007 — GERMANY DEFEND CROWN
Germany 2 Brazil 0
Hosts: China

Germany do not concede a single goal in their six matches in the tournament, thanks to goalkeeper Nadine Angerer, who saves a Marta penalty in Brazil women's first final. You'll never beat Nadine!

2011 — JAPAN JOY IS A FIRST
Japan 2 USA 2 (Japan win 3–1 on pens)
Hosts: Germany

Japan end a run of 25 games without beating USA to become the first Asian team to win the World Cup. Victory helps a grieving nation after an earthquake had killed thousands back home. Emotional!

2015 — THIRD TITLE FOR USA
USA 5 Japan 2
Hosts: Canada

The most astonishing start to a final saw USA 4–0 up after sixteen minutes, with Carli Lloyd scoring three of them. She is the second player to score a World Cup final hat-trick, her third goal an incredible strike from the halfway line. We love Lloyd's long-distance lob!

2019 — USA MAKE IT FOUR
USA 2 Netherlands 0
Hosts: France

USA beat Spain, France and England in the knockout rounds before top-scorer Megan Rapinoe's cool penalty sets up victory in the final. Rapinoe is player of the tournament and uses her global platform to campaign for social justice and equality. Megan on the march!

2023 — JOINTLY DOES IT
Final score:
Hosts: Australia and New Zealand

Australia and New Zealand are the first joint-hosts of the tournament. Please fill in the final score!

-THE SIX-
CONFEDERATIONS

These are the sporting bodies that run football's continental competitions.

Look at the map! Some countries are in the wrong confederation for their continent! Suriname and the Guyanas are geographically in South America, but play in CONCACAF because they enjoy closer ties to the Caribbean. Israel and Kazakhstan are in UEFA rather than AFC, and Australia moved from OFC to AFC in 2006 to play more competitive games.

FIFA has 211 members, but the confederations have 220! These extra nine teams are mostly from small island states who lack the resources to be full FIFA members or who are territorially part of France or the Netherlands. In addition, some nations are neither in FIFA nor a confederation, such as Vatican City, a sovereign state in Rome with a population of less than 500 people, and Western Sahara, a country in a territorial dispute with Morocco.

AFC (ASIAN FOOTBALL CONFEDERATION)
47 MEMBERS, 46 IN FIFA, INCLUDING SAUDI ARABIA, IRAN AND JAPAN

The countries covered by AFC make up 60 per cent of the entire world's population. South Korea is one of only five countries – and the only one from Asia – to qualify for the last ten consecutive World Cup tournaments. In 2002, they made history: after winning their first-ever World Cup match, they knocked out Italy and Spain to become the first Asian team to reach a World Cup semi-final. What a Korea high!

CAF (CONFEDERATION OF AFRICAN FOOTBALL)
54 MEMBERS, ALL IN FIFA, INCLUDING NIGERIA, GHANA AND EGYPT

Africa has more countries than any other continent, although CAF is only the second largest confederation because some European countries (such as the UK) have more than one national team. In total, thirteen African countries have qualified for the World Cup, including Angola, Togo and Zaire (now known as the Democratic Republic of Congo). Cabo Verde, which has a population of around 600,000, is the smallest of the 44 nations that have qualified for the Africa Cup of Nations. In 2013, they reached the quarter-finals. Verde good!

CONCACAF (CONFEDERATION OF NORTH, CENTRAL AMERICAN AND CARIBBEAN ASSOCIATION FOOTBALL)
41 MEMBERS, 35 IN FIFA, INCLUDING COSTA RICA, MEXICO AND USA

CONCACAF has produced more Women's World Cup-winners than any other confederation, thanks to the USA. The United States Women's National Team, known as USWNT, have won four world titles. In the first official World Cup in 1991, the matches were not shown in the USA and games were only 80 minutes long. By comparison, the 2019 Women's World Cup was broadcast in over 200 countries, and over 80 million people watched USA win the final. Explosive! US-TNT!

CONMEBOL (CONFEDERACIÓN SUDAMERICANA DE FÚTBOL)
10 MEMBERS, ALL IN FIFA, INCLUDING BRAZIL, ARGENTINA AND PERU

South America scores nine out of ten! Meaning that of the ten national teams in CONMEBOL, nine of them have played in World Cups. The one that hasn't is Venezuela, which holds the record for being the team that have reached the highest position – 25th – in the FIFA rankings, without ever qualifying for a World Cup. Yet in 2017, in one of the most unexpected runs in world football, the Venezuelan Under-20 side reached the final of the FIFA Under-20 World Cup, losing only 1–0 to England. You'd be Caracas not to think they will make it to a World Cup one day!

OFC (OCEANIA FOOTBALL CONFEDERATION)
13 MEMBERS, 11 IN FIFA, INCLUDING AMERICAN SAMOA, TONGA AND PAPUA NEW GUINEA

Oceania is home to some of the world's most isolated countries, set in the expanse of the Southern Pacific. Even arranging fixtures can be tough: which is why Tahiti winning the 2012 OFC Nations Cup, when ranked 179 in the world, was stunning. Tahiti beat New Zealand 1–0 in the final and qualified for the Confederations Cup, a competition that used to take place for the winners of the six continental championships. They played Nigeria, Spain and Uruguay, continental champions from around the world. Tahiti's government cancelled all work on the days of the matches so everyone could watch!

UEFA (UNION OF EUROPEAN FOOTBALL ASSOCIATIONS)
55 MEMBERS, ALL IN FIFA, INCLUDING ENGLAND, SPAIN AND ITALY

You all know about UEFA's best teams, such as France and Germany. But have you heard of San Marino – a landlocked country surrounded by Italy, with only a population of 30,000? Their football team is the lowest-ranked team in Europe, and has won only one match in their first 32 years of international football (1–0 against Liechtenstein in 2004). Yet they hold the record for the fastest-ever goal scored in a World Cup tie. That came, incredibly, after nine seconds against England in 1993. England went on to win the game 7–1, but that goal has never been forgotten. Mari-no, it hasn't!

-THE EUROS-

In 1960, seventeen national teams took part in the first European Championship. Now, every four years, over 50 men's and women's teams in UEFA battle to be crowned Europe's best. Here's a look at the winning teams.

⚬ WOMEN'S TEAMS ⚬

SWEDEN
1984

Sweden won the first tournament, in which each half was only 35 minutes, beating England on penalties. The winning penalty was scored by forward Pia Sundhage, who would go on to successfully manage USA, Sweden and Brazil. Pia power!

NORWAY
1987, 1993

Norway's first football tournament success since forming in 1902 came in 1987 on home soil thanks to a 2–1 win over neighbours Sweden. In 1993, they beat Italy 1–0 with a late goal from Birthe Hegstad, in what was their fourth consecutive final appearance. Hero Hegstad!

WEST GERMANY
1989

West Germany coasted through qualifying with eighteen goals scored and none conceded – including a 10–0 win over Switzerland. They beat Norway 4–1 in the final, starting a run of tremendous success for the country that would soon compete as a reunified Germany.

GERMANY 1991, 1995, 1997, 2001, 2005, 2009, 2013

In an incredible run of six straight tournament triumphs, between 1995 and 2013, Germany beat Sweden (twice), Norway (twice), Italy and England in finals. Forward and captain Birgit Prinz played in five of those finals, and won FIFA's World Player of the Year three times. Birgit was unbeatable!

NETHERLANDS
2017

Inspired by strike pairing Vivianne Miedema and Lieke Martens, the Netherlands came from behind to beat Denmark 4–2 in the final. They won every game and became the first hosts to win the competition since Germany in 2001. Dutch coach Sarina Wiegman masterminded success from the sideline.

ENGLAND
2022

England appointed Sarina Wiegman as coach and she guided them to their first major tournament victory after a 2–1 final win over Germany. Wiegman picked the same starting eleven for all six games and used her substitutes and tactical changes to maximum effect. England beat Norway 9–0, Spain 2–1 and Sweden 4–0 to reach the final, where they took the lead through sub Ella Toone's glorious lob. Germany equalized before another sub, Chloe Kelly, bundled home a deserved winning goal. She ripped off her shirt in joyous scenes as the whole country celebrated! Sub-lime!

MEN'S TEAMS

 SOVIET UNION
1960

The Soviet Union beat Yugoslavia 2–1 in the first final of what was then called the European Nations' Cup. The Soviet hero was their goalkeeper Lev Yashin, known as the Black Spider as he wore all-black kit. Smashin' Yashin!

 SPAIN
1964, 2008, 2012

Spain won their first trophy in 1964, beating the Soviet Union 2–1. They were also the first team to win back-to-back Euros, in 2008 and 2012, playing a possession-based game made in Barcelona. Barça brilliance brought it home!

 ITALY
1968, 2020

In 1968, Italy beat the Soviet Union in the semi-final after a coin toss – because the penalty shoot-out had not yet been invented – and then beat Yugoslavia 2–0 in the final. Italy won the 2020 tournament, beating England 3–2 on penalties in the final. Bravo!

 WEST GERMANY
1972, 1980

West Germany's top-scoring forward Gerd Müller was the hero in 1972, scoring two goals in the semi-final and the final, a 3–0 win over the Soviet Union. Eight years later, a last-minute winner clinched a 2–1 win over Belgium.

 CZECHOSLOVAKIA
1976

The Czechs won their first trophy after a dramatic penalty shoot-out against West Germany. Midfielder Antonín Panenka's innovative slow chipped penalty down the middle of the goal stunned the world and clinched victory. Now that penalty style is known as the Panenka. Perfection!

 FRANCE
1984, 2000

In 1984, France's four midfielders, known as *le carré magique*, or the magic square, inspired their first-ever trophy in a 2–0 final win over Spain. In 2000, *Les Bleus* needed an injury-time equalizer to force extra-time before a winner from David Trezeguet saw off Italy.

 NETHERLANDS
1988

Strikers Ruud Gullit and Marco van Basten scored a goal in each half in a 2–0 final win over Russia to seal the Netherlands' first-ever international trophy. Van Basten's goal, an incredible volley from a tight angle, remains one of the most famous, and best, goals in the competition's history. Van the Man!

 DENMARK
1992

This was one of the most astonishing triumphs in sporting history, as Denmark didn't even qualify for the tournament! They were given a place at the last minute after Yugoslavia were banned after a civil war broke up the country. Denmark, known as Danish Dynamite, beat Germany 2–0 in the final to seal the fairy tale. Boom!

 GERMANY
1996

In 1996, Germany beat England on penalties in the semi-final after Gareth Southgate, who went on to become the England coach, missed the decisive penalty. Germany beat the Czech Republic 1–0 in the final. The Germans were on the spot again!

 GREECE
2004

A major shock stunned the continent as unfancied Greece beat Portugal in the final. Greece showed you can win a tournament with a good defence, winning all their knockout matches 1–0 in a surprise triumph. These Greeks had no Achilles heel!

 PORTUGAL
2016

Portugal survived captain Cristiano Ronaldo being stretchered off injured in the final against France. With Ronaldo coaching the team from the sideline, Portugal won their first trophy – thanks to Eder's extra-time goal – and Ron went from agony to ecstasy!

-TROPHIES AND TITLES- ACROSS THE CONTINENTS

The other five confederations also have championships for their national teams, which usually take place every four years.

ASIAN CUP

Confederation: AFC
First held: Men's 1956; Women's 1975
Most wins: Men's Japan 4; Women's China 9

The AFC Women's Asian Cup is the oldest women's international football competition in the world. When it started in 1975, matches lasted 60 minutes. The tournament took place every two years, then three years and now it's every four years. Change is good! China won seven titles in a row from 1986 to 1999, and other winners include Thailand, North Korea and Japan.

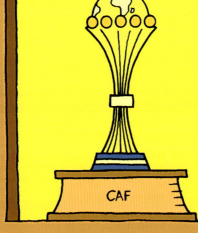

AFC

AFRICA CUP OF NATIONS

Confederation: CAF
First held: Men's 1957; Women's 1991
Most wins: Men's Egypt 7; Women's Nigeria 11

Egypt won the first two editions of the men's tournament, but had to wait until 1986 for a third success. After losing in the 1984 semi-final on a penalty shoot-out, they won six Africa Cup of Nations penalty shoot-outs in a row – including in the final against Cameroon (1986) and Ivory Coast (2006). In 2022, they reached another final, but lost 4–2 to Senegal – on penalties!

CAF

GOLD CUP

Confederation: CONCACAF
First held: Men's 1963; Women's 1991
Most wins: Men's Mexico 11; Women's USA 9

The men's competition is dominated by the two regional heavyweights, USA and Mexico. When Canada beat special guest Colombia to win the men's tournament in 2000, it was the only time since 1991 that either team failed to reach the final. The only two winners of the women's tournament, called CONCACAF W Championship, have been USA and Canada.

COPA AMÉRICA

Confederation: CONMEBOL
First held: Men's 1916; Women's 1991
Most wins: Men's Argentina and Uruguay 15; Women's Brazil 8

When Argentina won the 2021 men's Copa América, Lionel Messi was top scorer, top assist provider and won the tournament's best player award. Messi had inspired his team with a powerful speech in the dressing room before the final, and the 1–0 win over Brazil clinched Argentina their first trophy for 29 years. It was a long wait, but they got there thanks to marvellous Messi!

OFC NATIONS CUP

Confederation: OFC
First held: Men's 1973; Women's 1983
Most wins: Men's New Zealand 5; Women's New Zealand 6

In 2007, Australia left the OFC to compete in the AFC, which opened the door for other teams to challenge for titles. Since then, New Zealand have dominated, but Tahiti (men's tournament winners 2012) and Papua New Guinea (women's tournament winners 2022) have also triumphed in the region.

Between 1992 and 2017, FIFA held the Confederations Cup, a competition between each winner of their confederation's tournament. Brazil won the most titles (four), though in 2019 FIFA announced the tournament would no longer run.

-NATIONALITY-

Playing for your country is a great honour. Yet many players qualify for more than one national team. Here are FIFA's eligibility rules, and some players who swapped allegiances.

Originally, if a footballer wanted to play for a country's national team, they had to be a citizen of that country. FIFA's rules are now very different. If you want to play for a national football team, all you need is for one of the three following statements to be true:

✓ You were born in that country.

✓ At least one of your biological mother, father, grandmothers or grandfathers was born in that country.

(These two rules mean that if you were born in one country, and each of your grandparents were born in four other countries, you would have at least five national teams to choose from — if you are good enough, of course!)

✓ You have lived in that country for at least five years after the age of ten.

The rules also allow players to change national teams. If you have played for the national team of Country A, you are allowed to switch to Country B only if:

✓ You played for Country A in no more than three matches (including friendlies), none of which was in the World Cup or a continental competition (such as the Euros), and this all happened before you were 21.

This rule means that players who got a cap early in their careers for one country can change to play for another country when they are older. Players may want to do this for many reasons: they may have moved to the new country, they may want to play for a country that they feel more of a connection with, or they may want the opportunity to play for a country that has a greater chance of trophies!

At the 2022 World Cup, there were 137 players who were representing countries different from the country of their birth. That's about one in six players. The most common birth country was France, who had players born there and playing for Morocco, Spain, Germany, Tunisia, Senegal, Cameroon, Portugal, Ghana and Qatar.

DECISIONS, DECISIONS!

Here are some players who had tough choices to make about their national team:

SAM KERR

Born: Australia
Parents: Indian, Australian
Grandparents: Indian, Australian, Irish
Could have played for: Australia, India, Ireland
Played for: Australia

DECLAN RICE

Born: England
Parents: English
Grandparents: Irish
Could have played for: England, Ireland
Played for: Both! Ireland youth teams and three matches for Ireland aged 19. Switched to England aged 20.

ADNAN JANUZAJ

Born: Belgium
Parents: Kosovan, Albanian
Lived in: England for over five years
Could have played for: Belgium, Kosovo, Albania, England
Played for: Belgium

WILFRIED ZAHA

Born: Ivory Coast
Parents: Ivorian
Lived in: England from the age of four
Could have played for: Ivory Coast, England
Played for: Both! England youth teams, two friendly matches for England aged 21. Switched to Ivory Coast in 2017 aged 24.

Taulant Xhaka (left) and Granit Xhaka (right) at Euro 2016

BROTHERS TAULANT AND GRANIT XHAKA

Born: Switzerland
Parents: Kosovan, Albanian
Could have played for: Switzerland, Kosovo, Albania
Played for: Taulant played for Switzerland youth teams before switching to Albania aged 23. Granit played for Switzerland. The brothers played against each other in Euro 2016, Switzerland beating Albania 1–0.

Thiago Alcântara (left) and Rafinha Alcântara (right)

BROTHERS THIAGO AND RAFINHA ALCÂNTARA

Born: Italy (Thiago), Brazil (Rafinha)
Parents: Brazilian
Lived in: Spain
Could have played for: Italy, Brazil, Spain
Played for: Thiago moved to Spain aged five and played for their youth teams before making his senior Spain debut in 2011. Rafinha played for Spain Under-19s but, aged 20, switched to Brazil, with whom their father Mazinho had won the 1994 World Cup.

Tuesday

Alex

Hello from the home of the "hallowed turf"! That's what fans call the pitch at Wembley. England's national stadium, which Pelé called the "cathedral of football", has been the most famous stadium in the world for a century. It hosted the 1966 World Cup final, as well as the 1996 and 2020 men's Euros finals and the 2022 women's Euros final. It has also hosted seven European Cup and Champions Leagues finals, more than anywhere else. It's the biggest stadium in the UK, with a capacity of 90,000. An arching glory!

10:20 AM ✓✓

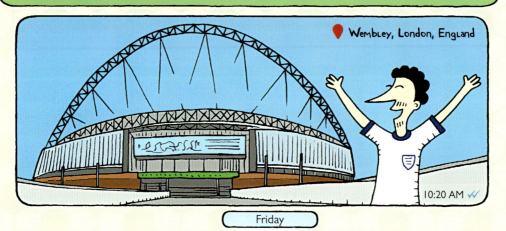

Wembley, London, England

10:20 AM ✓✓

Friday

Ben

Greetings from Glasgae! Hampden Park, the Scottish national stadium, is a monster (but not of a Loch Ness variety!). It was the world's largest stadium from 1903 to 1950, when it handed the title to the Maracanã in Rio de Janeiro, Brazil. It broke attendance records for matches many times, and its home crowd of 149,416 for Scotland v. England in 1937 is still the biggest attendance at a match anywhere in Europe. Capacity is now 51,866.

1:15 PM ✓✓

Hampden Park, Glasgow, Scotland

1:15 PM

Sunday

Alex

Bonjour, mon ami! I'm in Paris, the city of lights. It should be renamed the city of floodlights! France's national stadium is an architectural wonder to rival the Eiffel Tower. Built to host the 1998 World Cup final, it has an instantly recognizable circular roof, which appears to hover over the stands. As well as being the French football team's home ground, the Stade de France is also where the national rugby team play and is the venue of the 2024 Olympic Games. *Magnifique!*

12:42 PM

📍 Stade de France, Paris, France

12:42 PM

Today

Ben

Hi, Alex! I mean "high", Alex! At an altitude of 2,200m above sea level, the Azteca is the highest stadium to have hosted a World Cup final. It was also the first stadium to host two World Cup finals, in 1970 and 1986. It has hosted some of the World Cup's most memorable games: the 1970 final, when Pelé's super-stylish Brazil defeated Italy, and the 1986 semi-final between Argentina and England, when Maradona scored both his Hand of God goal and the Goal of Century, dribbling through the England defence. Az-tekkers!

3:02 PM

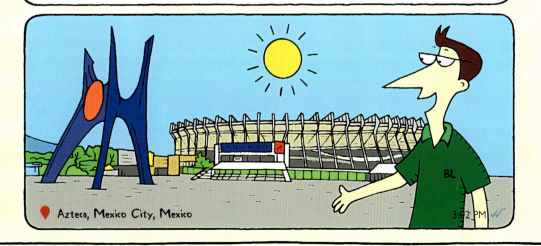

📍 Azteca, Mexico City, Mexico

3:02 PM

-PLAY OUR WAY-

The rules of football are the same everywhere, but the style in which the game is played differs around the world. Here are five countries famous for their unique approach.

BRAZIL

Ever since Brazil won their first World Cup in 1958, the national team has been known for their joyful playing style, based on flamboyance, creativity and dazzling technical skills. Brazilians consider their best players, such as Pelé, Ronaldinho and Neymar, as artists, capable of creating beauty on the pitch. One reason Brazilian players are so skilful is that ever since the 1950s, Brazilian children tend to begin their football careers playing futsal – indoor five-a side football with a small, heavy ball – which emphasizes speed, accuracy and ball control. The result is that Brazil is a factory of top players with amazing technical ability, self-confidence and improvisational skills. It also helps that Brazil is the country of samba, a style of dance that develops great flexibility in the hips. This hip flexibility makes Brazilian footballers particularly good dribblers and explains why they pioneered acrobatic moves like the bicycle kick. Their hips don't lie!

USA WOMEN

The USWNT has won the Women's World Cup more times than any other team – partly due to their willingness never to give up. Some of their most famous results have come against the odds: in 2011, they scored the latest goal in World Cup history in a quarter-final win over Brazil; and in 2012, the latest goal in Olympic history after coming back three times to beat Canada 4–3. Their attitude came out of necessity: in the team's early years, players hardly made any money from playing, so were driven by their desire to represent their country and open up opportunities to future generations. The current team has continued this tenacity on the pitch and created a better future off it; the 2019 World Cup-winning team successfully campaigned for equal pay with the men's team, and became well known for standing up for social justice. This team are fighters on and off the pitch!

URUGUAY

Uruguay are arguably football's most overachieving nation. They have a population of only 3.5 million, a fraction of the size of their neighbours Argentina (45 million) and Brazil (212 million). Yet Uruguay are tied with Argentina for the most number of Copa América titles and they have won the World Cup twice, by far the smallest nation ever to be world champions. Uruguayans say their secret is *garra charrúa*, which loosely translates as the grit of the Charrúa, who were the Indigenous people who lived in the area where Uruguay is now. The Charrúa fought against the Spanish settlers and lost, but their bravery in the face of defeat has become part of Uruguayan national identity. Uruguayan players tend to be physical and tough, with a never-say-die mentality. They have a deep belief that, whoever the opposition, there is always a chance they can win. Thanks to their *garra charrúa*, they often do!

NETHERLANDS

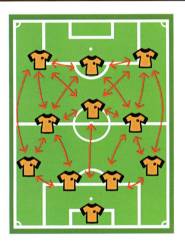

The Netherlands are a team from a middle-sized European country that have had a massive influence on how football is played. In the late 1960s, Ajax coach Rinus Michels and player Johan Cruyff invented a theory called Total Football, in which players could swap positions. Total Football helped Ajax win three consecutive European Cups and the Netherlands reach two World Cup finals in the 1970s. Since then, Dutch players have often starred in Europe's top teams, and their tactical know-how has spread across the Continent. You can never write off the Netherlands!

ITALY

Italy cherish defensive play more than any other nation; after all, the captain of their first World Cup-winning team in 1934, Gianpiero Combi, was a goalkeeper. In the 1940s, player-turned-manager Gipo Viani watched fishermen get ready for work at a harbour. He noticed that behind their main net, they put out another net as a back-up. This gave him an idea: put in an extra defender, known as a sweeper, behind the defence, to make sure no goals were conceded. This defensive system became known as *catenaccio*, meaning "padlock". As well as being a style of play, it was also a mindset: that to not concede a goal was the most important thing. One of Italy's most beloved football writers even said the ideal game would always finish 0–0, because it meant both defences had been perfect.

-NICKNAMES OF NATIONAL TEAMS-

Many nations have animal nicknames, usually from native species or heraldic symbols.

The animals in the picture all appear in national team nicknames. Usually, the team are known as that animal, such as The Eagle-Owls, but sometimes the nickname is more specific, such as The Lions of Teranga (Senegal).

	ANIMAL	COUNTRY
1.	Canary	Brazil
2.	Cheetah	Benin, Iran
3.	Coelacanth	Comoros
4.	Crocodile	Lesotho, Timor-Leste
5.	Dragon	Bosnia-Herzegovina, China, Wales
6.	Eagle	Albania, Mali, Poland, Serbia, Syria, Tunisia, UAE
7.	Eagle-owl	Finland
8.	Elephant	Ivory Coast
9.	Falcons	Montenegro, Saudi Arabia
10.	Fennec fox	Algeria
11.	Giant sable antelope	Angola
12.	Jaguar	Belize
13.	Leopard	DR Congo, Kazakhstan, Zanzibar
14.	Lion	Afghanistan, Bulgaria, Cameroon, Cuba, England, Iraq, Morocco, Senegal
15.	Panther	Gabon
16.	Parrot	Dominica
17.	Sparrow hawk	Togo
18.	Stallion	Burkina Faso
19.	Street dog	Philippines
20.	Tiger	Malaysia
21.	Turtle	Cayman Islands
22.	Wasp	Brunei, Rwanda
23.	Wolf	Latvia
24.	Zebra	Botswana

-THE COUNTRIES- QUIZ

1. **In 1904, seven countries got together to set up FIFA as a way of organizing international football. Which country was not in the original group of seven?**

   a) England

   b) France

   c) Spain

   d) Denmark

2. **What do the following countries have in common: Italy, Netherlands, Australia and Japan?**

   a) They all started playing in one confederation and moved to another.

   b) Their national team kit is a different colour to their national flag.

   c) Their national anthem has no words in it.

   d) They have all won trophies with an English coach.

3. **Match the country to the continents in which they play.**

1) Thailand	a) Oceania
2) Tunisia	b) Europe
3) Turkey	c) Asia
4) Puerto Rico	d) North America
5) Papua New Guinea	e) South America
6) Peru	f) Africa

4. **What football record does San Marino hold?**

   a) The lowest-ranked team in Europe

   b) Won only one match in their first 32 years

   c) Fastest-ever goal in a World Cup match, scored after nine seconds against England

   d) All of the above

5. **England won the 2022 Women's Euros by beating Germany 2–1 in the final. What did coach Sarina Wiegman do before all six games in the tournament?**

   a) She picked the same starting eleven.

   b) She correctly predicted the result.

   c) She ran three laps around the pitch.

   d) She told a joke in Dutch as part of her pre-match team-talk.

6. **Match the animal to the national team nickname.**

1) Eagle	a) Morocco
2) Elephant	b) Poland
3) Panther	c) Gabon
4) Lion	d) Ivory Coast

7. **Which stadium has hosted the most European Cup and Champions League finals?**

   a) Wembley Stadium, London

   b) Stade de France, Paris

   c) Camp Nou, Barcelona

   d) Azteca Stadium, Mexico City

8. **Players born in which country were the most common at the 2022 World Cup?**

   a) England

   b) Netherlands

   c) Brazil

   d) France

9. **The first World Cup final in 1930 was notable for a row between finalists Uruguay and Argentina over what?**

   a) The referee

   b) The half-time snack

   c) The ball

   d) The kick-off time

10. **Which team has won the Women's World Cup the most times?**

    a) Norway

    b) Germany

    c) Japan

    d) USA

Answers: 1. a, 2. b, 3. 1) c, 2) f, 3) b, 4) d, 5) a, 6) e, 4. d, 5. a, 6. 1) b, 2) d, 3) c, 4) a, 7. a, 8. d, 9. c, 10. d

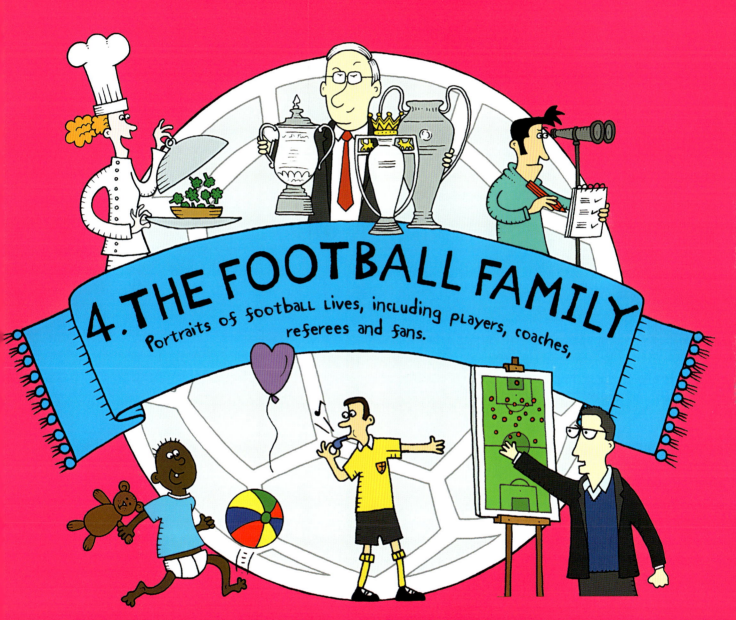

4. THE FOOTBALL FAMILY

Portraits of football lives, including players, coaches, referees and fans.

-THE EARLY YEARS-

You're never too young to start your football adventure. Here we chart the journey from birth, through the English academy system, to becoming a professional player.

AGE 0 TO 7

For young footballers aged seven or below, the only option is what's called "grassroots" football. This refers to the thousands of groups that organize coaching sessions and games for children of all ages and levels, often in community centres or local parks. It is called "grassroots" football because these loosely-organized, community-run groups are the base of the whole football structure, just like lots of underground roots are the base of shiny and visible blades of grass.

TOP OF THE GRASS

Phil Foden: spotted by Manchester City aged five, who connected him, aged seven, to grassroots club Reddish Vulcans.
Harry Kane: played for Ridgway Rovers Under-7s in Chingford, East London.

AGE 8 TO 10

Almost every professional club in the UK has an academy, which is a programme to discover and develop young talent. Academies are allowed to sign up the best local grassroots talent aged eight or above. On average, there are about 120 players per academy, from Under-9s to Under-21s, when the academy system finishes. That means that around 10,000 people are in the academy system at any one time. The first four years at an academy are called the foundation phase and involve:

★ Playing 5 v. 5, 7 v. 7 and 9 v. 9
★ Training after school a couple of times a week
★ Playing matches on weekends
★ Living within a one-hour journey from the club

SCOUT AND ABOUT

A person who watches football games in order to look for promising players is called a scout. The big clubs each have networks of up to 50 scouts (many are volunteers) across the country who spend their weekends watching grassroots football games and recommending players. If you are a good grassroots player, who plays in local tournaments, you will almost certainly be observed by a scout at some stage. We asked a Premier League scout what they were looking for. He said: "Showing good technical promise, speed of thought and effort: you might not be the most talented player, but if you can apply yourself well, and if, when you make a mistake, you work hard to put it right, that could be a deciding factor."

WHAT ARE THE CHANCES?

If you get into an academy, the chances of turning professional are still low. A 2022 survey of male players aged between 21 and 26, who had been at the academies of top clubs, showed that only 3 in 10 had signed professional contracts, and only 1 in 10 had made more than 20 appearances in the top four tiers of the English league. Don't give up the day job!

AGE 11 TO 15

The next four years of the academy system are called the youth development phase. Players can be released from an academy, or join an academy, at any stage. This phase involves:

★ Playing 11 v. 11
★ Training after school a couple of times a week
★ Playing matches on weekends
★ Living within a 90-minute journey from the club

AGE 16 TO 20

The final years of the academy are called the professional development phase and involve:

★ Players being given "scholarships", which are two-year contracts, for which the player receives a salary. All scholarship players must go to college to study for at least one day a week.
★ Training during the day, four days a week
★ Playing matches on weekends
★ Moving to live near the club if they are not local

LION CUBS RULE

Even though the FA runs national teams from Under-15s for men and Under-16s for women, the big competitions only begin at Under-17 level. FIFA runs an Under-17 and an Under-20 World Cup every two years for both men and women. England men won both trophies in 2017.

OTHER PATHS

Some top pros make it without going through the academy system.

Troy Deeney: left school at sixteen to become a bricklayer and joined his local non-league club in Birmingham. Aged eighteen, he joined League Two team Walsall and four years later moved to Watford. He captained the Hornets in their promotion to the Premier League and became a club legend, scoring 140 goals in more than 400 appearances.

Jamie Vardy: joined Sheffield Wednesday's academy as a child but was let go aged sixteen. He played for non-league teams until age 25, then he was signed by Leicester City in the Premier League and in 2015 was called up by England.

-A FOOTBALLER'S LIFE-

Footballers spend most of their working hours preparing for matches at their training ground. Their daily schedules include the following elements:

HEALTH CHECK
15 minutes

Players get a morning health check-up when they arrive at the training ground. This involves giving a blood or urine sample to measure heart-rate, hydration levels and overall health. The players complete a digital wellness questionnaire which factors in their diet and sleep. In some cases, it alerts the medical team to a player at risk of injury, and therefore changes that player's schedule for the day (for example, no sprinting).

GYM WORK
Up to 90 minutes

Players have to be super-fit – and stay that way! That can mean two gym sessions per day: the first before the morning training session, known as "pre-activation", to wake up the muscles and ready the body for training; the second session, in the afternoon, might be lighter, to warm down the muscles. Players may have their own individual programme of exercises to complete, depending on their physical condition. They also get massages before and after training.

TACTICAL ANALYSIS
Up to 20 minutes

Team: The coach speaks to the whole team to go through what worked and what didn't work in the previous match, using video clips to illustrate points. The coach explains what the targets are for the next training session and the tactics that the team will deploy for the next match. These tactical sessions are short as the coach does not want to overload the players with too much information to remember.

Up to 40 minutes

Individual: Some clubs have individual development or performance coaches, who sit down with players for a one-on-one video analysis session. They break down the player's performance, looking at their decision-making, positioning, body shape and movement, highlighting areas to improve. The best players are those who listen to the feedback and use it to play even better.

TRAINING
Up to 90 minutes

Out on the training ground at last – and with a ball at their feet! This session lasts between 75 and 90 minutes and involves different drills – sometimes up to six of them. Each one has a clear learning objective and tactical reason behind it, always linked to the coach's ultimate game-plan. These might include smaller-sided drills to keep possession in tight spaces, distribution from defence, zonal marking, one-on-one duels and reacting quickly to losing the ball. The session ends with a short eleven-a-side game to put what has been learned into action. If the fixture list is not too busy, some coaches might put on a second, shorter, training session in the afternoon. That's all the football work for the day!

COMMUNITY WORK
Up to 2 hours

With some afternoons free, players often represent their clubs by visiting schools, hospitals or charities to support the local community. Some players love meeting new people, learning about new skills and working with kids.

THE MATCH-DAY ROUTINE

Have you ever wondered how players get ready for a big game? This is the timetable for match day, with a 3 p.m. kick-off.

AWAY GAME PROCEDURE

18:00 The team arrive at a hotel the night before.

HOME GAME PROCEDURE

8:00 The players wake up in their own beds.

11:00 Attend a team meeting at the hotel or training ground.

13:00 Travel together to the stadium.

14:00 Get changed and start warming up, which continues on the pitch.

14:50 The coach gives the final team-talk.

15:00 The match kicks off.

-FOOD AND- NUTRITION

In order to perform at their best, footballers must eat the right foods at the right time. Their diet provides them with energy, as well as vitamins and minerals that are important to stay healthy. The menu below was prepared by Craig Umenyi, who has worked as a nutritionist for Premier League clubs. It provides a footballer with all their nutritional needs before a big match.

In a bite: focus on proteins for muscle health.

MENU

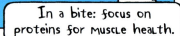

2 DAYS BEFORE A MATCH

Breakfast   Veggie omelette with two slices of wholegrain bread

Lunch   Chicken breast, pasta with tomato sauce, asparagus and side salad
Low-fat Greek yoghurt with fruit

Afternoon snack   Protein shake
Omega-3 supplement
Chicken wrap

Dinner   Salmon fillet, portion of rice and grilled vegetables
No pudding

Nutritionist's notes:

Protein maintains and repairs muscle. Good sources are meat, fish, eggs and dairy. Over a long season some players will struggle to maintain their muscle mass, so I make sure their diet is rich in proteins a few days before a match. Vegetables provide vitamins and minerals, which are good for the immune system. The Omega-3 supplement helps the body recover after exercise.

In a bite: stock up on SLOW carbohydrates.

MENU

1 DAY BEFORE A MATCH

Breakfast Porridge with fruit
Glass of milk

Lunch Noodle soup
Chicken, with sweet potato
wedges, salad and vegetables
Smoothie

Afternoon snack Tuna and light-mayo
sandwich

Dinner Slices of bread with
balsamic vinegar
Spaghetti bolognese
with 0% fat beef mince
Rice pudding

Nutritionist's notes:
Today is the day footballers eat the most food. Most of the energy we get comes from carbohydrates, especially the starchy kind like potatoes, rice, pasta, oats and grains. The body takes a day or so to process these foods, so players stock up a day before the game. To make meals more interesting, we disguise different carbs in the same meal. Rice pudding is a winner!

In a bite: light lunch and faster carbohydrates.

MENU

MATCH DAY

Breakfast Cornflakes, low-fat Greek yoghurt
Two slices of toast with jam
Fruit smoothie with milk

Lunch Fillet of sea bass and portion of rice
Glass of water containing an
electrolyte tablet

Before game Either a gel, a sports drink, a
banana or a cereal bar

Nutritionist's notes:
I aim for the players to have as much energy during the match as possible, but also to feel light on their feet. Fatty foods are a no-no since they make the stomach feel heavy. Sports drinks, gels and fruit contain carbs that the body can turn into energy fast, so one of these is taken shortly before the game. Electrolyte tablets contain salts which replenish the salts players lose through sweating.

-REST AND RECOVERY-

Footballers play so many matches over a season that looking after their bodies to maintain fitness and avoid injury is an increasingly important part of their routine. The methods below prepare players for games and aid recuperation afterwards.

YOGA

Yoga is a combination of physical poses, breathing techniques and meditation which help the body and mind. Yoga improves players' flexibility, strength, endurance and balance. It can also prevent injuries to the hips and spine, which are often imbalanced because players have a preferred kicking foot and standing foot. Most clubs now use yoga as a recovery tool, and Germany used a yoga coach to help them win the 2014 World Cup. Ja-ga!

MASSAGE

Massage is when a qualified therapist rubs or kneads muscles in the body with their hands. It can treat specific pain or be very calming and ease stress. Players have massages before a match to wake up and stimulate the muscles to increase power. They have massages after a match to reduce post-exercise soreness and restore the blood flow to tight muscles. Now relaaaax!

HYDROTHERAPY

The use of water for recovery takes many forms. Cold- and hot-water immersions (known as contrast-water immersions) reduce muscle tightness after a match. Aqua-jogging, which involves running on a treadmill underwater, aids recovery from serious injury. Being in water eliminates up to 90 per cent of body weight, so players can run without bearing their own weight. The England team have their own hydrotherapy pool complete with adjustable floors and an underwater treadmill. Swim time!

CRYOTHERAPY

From the Greek words for cold (*kruos*) and healing (*therapeia*), cryotherapy is a relatively new recovery method used by top clubs. After training and matches, players wear a hat, shorts, socks and gloves and stand in a chamber exposed to icy temperatures as low as -150ºC for up to three minutes. The cold is thought to reduce the inflammation and muscle soreness that come after exercise. It also stimulates the release of feel-good chemicals in the body. Cryotherapy has replaced ice baths (which last longer) as players' preferred cold cure. *Brrrrr* – do not try this at home!

COMPRESSION

To aid recovery, players wear skin-tight garments – usually leggings, but sometimes socks or sleeves – that cling to the body and reduce muscle vibration while moving. They can be worn during, or up to 48 hours after, exercise. Compression works by narrowing the veins, so blood flows faster to the heart, which pumps it back to aching muscles, reducing soreness and fatigue. Some players are recommended to sleep in compression wear so the benefits can work overnight. Easy squeezy!

SLEEP

Sleep is very important to good performance and a critical part of recovery. Players who sleep deeply for long stretches have quicker reaction times, clearer judgement and decision-making skills than those who don't sleep well. Good sleep also allows players to form stronger memories and learn fast, as the brain makes connections while asleep. Longer sleep also helps players ease pain. Some clubs provide beds at the training ground for afternoon naps and a sleep coach who will help a player choose the best mattress. Sweet dreamzzzzzz…

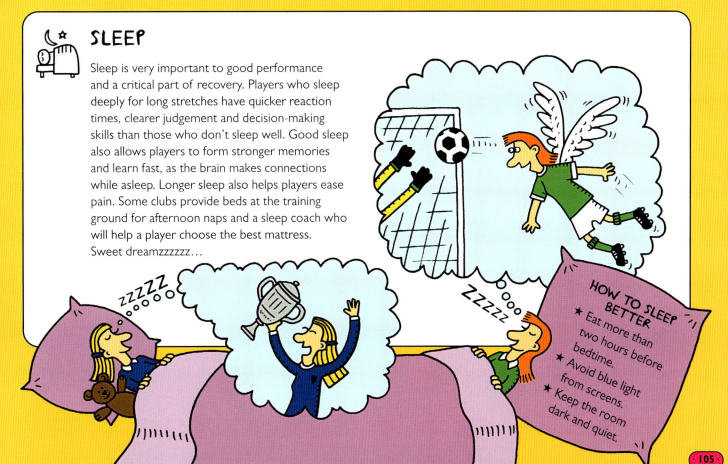

HOW TO SLEEP BETTER
* Eat more than two hours before bedtime.
* Avoid blue light from screens.
* Keep the room dark and quiet.

⚽ -THE COACH- ⚽

The coach's role is to improve the players, select the tactics and talk to the media. Our celebration of coaches starts with a look at some of the best ever!

BRITS ABROAD

Organized football was established in the UK before other countries, and at the start of the last century, British coaches went to Europe to spread their football knowledge.

One of the first was **William Garbutt**, who coached many Italian teams between 1912 and 1948. He led Genoa to their only league success, in 1924, and has been called the most important man in Italian football history. His players called him "mister", a term that Italian players still call their coaches today. *Ciao, mister!*

Vic Buckingham was another travelling Brit. In the 1960s and 1970s, he established the possession-based playing philosophy still in place at Ajax and Barcelona and gave Dutch player Johan Cruyff, who would become one of football's most influential thinkers (see the opposite page), his debut at Ajax. Vic-tory!

FOREIGN MASTERS

In the second half of the last century, it became easier to travel, and therefore exchange ideas and theories. At this point, European coaches started developing their own methods to win matches.

Valeriy Lobanovskyi was a Ukrainian coach who, in the 1970s and 1980s, made Dynamo Kyiv Eastern Europe's most successful team. He used science and statistics to calculate the positions that would lead to most scoring opportunities.

Arsène Wenger was a French coach who won trophies in France, Japan and England, as Arsenal's most successful coach. He introduced modern training to English football and won three Premier League titles, including in 2001, when Arsenal went unbeaten. Invincible!

BEST OF BRITISH

Later in the twentieth century, elite coaches were working throughout the world, yet Great Britain continued to produce some of football's most successful coaches.

Brian Clough was one of them. Outspoken and innovative, Clough led Derby and Nottingham Forest from the second division to the first division league title. He also conquered Europe with Forest, winning stunning back-to-back European Cup victories in 1979 and 1980.

The most successful British coach of all time is **Sir Alex Ferguson**. He was successful in Scotland before taking over at Manchester United, where between 1986 and 2013, he won thirteen Premier League titles. Ferguson was a great communicator and always open to changing his ideas, even in times of success. His total trophy count is over 50 – that requires a big cabinet!

MOST INFLUENTIAL COACHES

The most influential coaches spread their message by coaching players who then become coaches themselves. Here are three coaches whose legacy continues through the tactics and ideas of the generation of coaches they taught.

JOHAN CRUYFF

Coached 1985–2013

The former Ajax, Barcelona and Netherlands winger set up an institute in his name which now teaches his methods to coaches across the world. The hallmarks of a Cruyff team are a combination of possession, movement, rotating positions and using the full pitch. He influenced:

 Xabi Alonso   Mikel Arteta
 Luis Enrique   Pep Guardiola
 Erik ten Hag   Xavi Hernández
 Kasper Hjulmand   Ronald Koeman
 Julen Lopetegui  Sarina Wiegman

MARCELO BIELSA

Coached 1982 – present

The understated Argentine has inspired over 160 of his former players to become coaches. His high-tempo attacking style requires stamina, bravery, concentration, improvisation and precise tactical preparation, all of which he hones during intense training sessions. He influenced:

 Matías Almeyda   Carlos Corberán
 Marcelo Gallardo   Gabriel Heinze
Gerardo Martino   Mauricio Pochettino
 Lionel Scaloni   Diego Simeone
 Jorge Sampaoli   Roberto de Zerbi

RALF RANGNICK

Coached 1983 – present

Rangnick's counter-pressing tactic, when players win back the ball within seven seconds of losing it, was credited with helping Germany win the 2014 World Cup. His football theories have inspired a generation of coaches now working at Europe's top clubs. He influenced:

 Ralph Hasenhüttl   Adi Hütter
 Matthias Jaissle Jesse Marsch
 Julian Nagelsmann   Marco Rose
 Roger Schmidt Domenico Tedesco
 Thomas Tuchel David Wagner

-A GUIDE TO TACTICS-

The coach decides on the style of play. They choose the tactics (such as the ones listed below) and the formation (such as the ones opposite) to give their team the best chance of winning. Sometimes they might switch style or formation during a game. Any style can go with any formation. Mix and match!

⚽ POSSESSION GAME

Technically excellent players keep the ball with short intricate passing combinations, while speedy and smart attackers create space with their constant movement. The goalkeeper often acts as a sweeper, the defenders can move into midfield and the midfielders ensure the team has over 60 per cent possession in the match. If the opposition doesn't have the ball, they can't score.
Used by: Pep Guardiola (won league titles with Manchester City, Barcelona and Bayern Munich)

⚽ HIGH PRESS

This focuses on the idea that the higher up the pitch you win the ball, the closer you are to the opposition goal. It's tiring because all outfield players need to work together to constantly "press" the opposition on the ball, starting with the strikers, who need to be energetic and unselfish. Once you win back the ball, you should already be close to goal – now shoot!
Used by: Jürgen Klopp (won league titles with Liverpool and Borussia Dortmund)

⚽ LONG BALL

This style involves playing long passes from the back to a tall striker, who can hold up the ball and start an attack by passing to other players, either a winger or attacking midfielder. This requires defensive stability, wingers who can attack and defend and a target striker able to control the ball – as well as players who can kick the ball a long way.
Used by: Sean Dyche (helped Burnley stay in the Premier League for five seasons and qualify for Europe)

⚽ COUNTER-ATTACK

The opposition are encouraged to push players forward with the ball. The aim is to win back the ball and then, at top speed, launch an attack to exploit the space while opposition players are out of position. Players need to move the ball forward at speed, with midfielders who can make accurate long passes and rapid strikers to take advantage. It can be risky, but when it works, it's effective!
Used by: Antonio Conte (won league titles with Chelsea, Juventus and Internazionale)

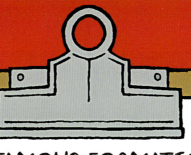

SIX FAMOUS FORMATIONS

4–4–2

The two strikers each provide a goal threat, which keeps both centre-backs occupied, while the wide midfielders and full-backs stretch the pitch to its full width. English coaches used to love this formation, but it's not as popular now.

4–2–3–1

The two midfielders form a solid base known as a double pivot, while players around them create angles and triangles to help passing. The player behind the centre-forward has the freedom to create lots of chances!

4–3–3

The wide attackers in this formation bring extra goal-power and put pressure on opposition full-backs to stay in their own half, while a third midfielder can provide an extra player in the central areas, where keeping the ball is key.

3–5–2

The third centre-back offers extra protection and can start attacks. The wing-backs play as full-backs *and* wingers, so need to be fast and tactically aware – they can be the star players on this team!

3–4–3

This has a bit of everything, with three centre-backs, a midfield double pivot and two wing-backs for attacking width. This offers up to five players in attack and still leaves cover against a counter-attack.

4–1–4–1

This needs a brilliant defensive midfielder who can block off opposition moves and launch attacks as a creative playmaker. This flexi-formation can switch to 4–3–3 when attacking and 4–5–1 when defending.

-THE MENTAL GAME-

The coach also works on helping their players respond to different situations in the best possible way. Here is how a coach could help their players with their mental performance in three key areas.

RESILIENCE

I need to build my players' resilience so they respond in a positive way to both good and bad things.

During a game a player scores an own goal.

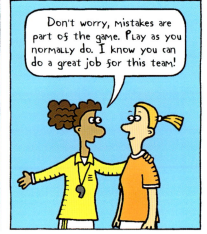
Don't worry, mistakes are part of the game. Play as you normally do. I know you can do a great job for this team!

COMPOSURE

I want my players to stay composed so they will be calm and make good decisions under pressure.

There's a last-minute penalty to win the game.

Keep calm; take deep breaths! Remember you have practised this, so focus on your technique. You've got this!

COMMITMENT

I love it when my players show commitment: by working hard to learn and improve whatever the conditions.

It starts to pour with rain at training.

One more lap to go! This will help build your fitness for the next game; keep going and stay strong!

LESSONS IN LEADERSHIP

Coaches use their leadership skills to improve the performance of their players. With the right words, a coach can inspire individuals in any team to fulfil their potential and reach their goals.

MOTIVATION

COMPASSION

SUPPORT

-THE REFEREE-

The referee is the person in charge of a game of football. Their responsibilities include making sure the match starts at the right time, enforcing the rules and maintaining discipline. It's a tough gig!

WHO ARE YA, REF?

Peeep! If you are fourteen years old or over, you can become a referee. The first step is to take the FA Referee Course, which involves 90 minutes of online learning and 11 hours of training. You will qualify as a ref after you have taken charge of five games organized by your local county's FA. England has about 28,000 registered referees and about 4,000 take the ref's course every year.

Once you are qualified, you will start refereeing at the lowest level of county leagues. If you enjoy it and are good you will get promoted to higher leagues. Referees at the top level, officiating matches in the Premier League and the Championship, are professionals, meaning that it is their full-time job. Yet even the best-paid referees in the Premier League earn less in a year than the top footballers earn in a week. *Peeep! Peeep!*

FAB FOUR

Referees work in teams of four:
  ★ The referee, who is always on the pitch
  ★ Two assistant referees, who are positioned on each touchline, to help judge offsides
  ★ The fourth official, who is off the pitch, usually near the technical area, and helps to manage substitutions

Referees must always carry:

1. Coin: flipped at the beginning of the match to decide which side kicks off

2. Whistle: used to start and stop play

3. Watch: to keep time

4. Notebook: to write down important incidents in the game

5. Yellow and red cards: for disciplining players

BOSS IN BLACK

Early referees looked very smart. John Langenus, who officiated the first World Cup final in 1930, wore a blazer, shirt, tie and plus fours! Traditionally referees always wore black shirts, shorts and socks – to distinguish them from the colourful shirts used by teams – but this changed in the 1990s. Now refs' shirts vary between many bright colours, but their shorts and socks are always black.

ONLY HUMAN

Referees are trained to be as fair as possible. When we look at averages, research shows a referee may be influenced without realizing it by factors such as the size of players or pressure from the crowd.
  ★ Shorter refs give more cards than taller refs.
  ★ Refs are more likely to punish taller players for fouling shorter players, than vice versa.
  ★ If after 90 minutes the score difference between two teams is a single goal, refs will add more extra time than if the score difference was two or more goals, especially if the losing team are a bigger team.

John Langenus: suited and booted

HAVING A WORD WITH THE REF

We spoke to Darren England, a Premier League referee who has also taken charge of international games.

When did you realize you wanted to be a referee, and what was it that you found appealing about the role?

I first realized I wanted to be a referee when I knew I was not going to make it as a professional footballer. It was kind of a back-up plan. I like the fact that every game is different and you are working under high pressure, making decisions in a matter of seconds.

What are the skills that you need to be a good referee?

You have to be a good leader of your own team of officials and also the players, managers and the fans. You have to be able to manage people. You have to be resilient, as lots of people question your ability! Communication is a key skill, not just with words but also with your body language, which is what most people see on TV and in the stadiums.

How much time do you spend training?

I train around 5–6 days per week, as we have to be as fit as the players to keep up with the game!

Did you have another job before becoming a professional referee, and if so what was it?

I was also a football coach when I started refereeing. I coached for my local and favourite team, Barnsley. I used to coach the young, talented footballers in the academy and also deliver projects in the local community using the power of football to make people's lives better.

What is the hardest part of the job?

Making sure you do not make a mistake that impacts the outcome of the match. This is the worst thing for us.

How do you cope with the pressure of refereeing in a big match?

I try to prepare the same way for every match, which is to stay calm and relaxed. During the match I remain very focused and just take each decision I need to make, one at a time! I do not worry about past decisions in the game as it is all about the next decision!

What's your favourite part of the job?

Knowing that you can contribute positively to each game! Being part of memorable matches and memorable goals is also a great feeling. We have the next best view to the players, remember!

MEET THE SUPERFANS

When it comes to football lives, we can't forget the fans. These colourful characters are as keen as they come!

CHRISTIAN KINNER

Borussia Dortmund fan Christian holds the world record for the longest football shout. He belted out "*Tor*" (German for "goal") for 43.56 seconds at a sound level above 80 decibels (about as loud as a lawnmower). *Tor*-iffic!

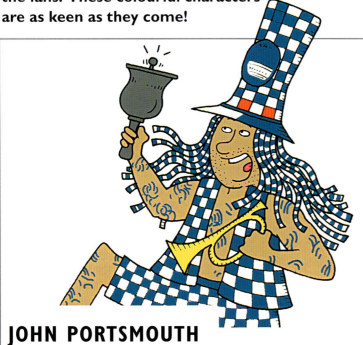

JOHN PORTSMOUTH FOOTBALL CLUB WESTWOOD

A bookseller by day, this superfan transforms himself during Pompey games. He wears a top hat and wig, and gets the crowd going by playing a bugle and ringing a handbell. John officially changed his middle names to the name of the club, and he has PFC engraved on his teeth. We love the way he sup-PORTS – and what a MOUTH!

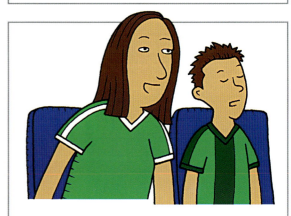

SILVIA GRECCO

When Brazilian mum Silvia takes her blind and autistic son Nickollas to watch his club Palmeiras, she narrates every moment of the game for him so as to make the experience as exciting as possible. For this she won the FIFA Fan Award in 2019.

MARGARITA LUENGO

Margarita has placed a bouquet of red and white carnations by the corner flag at Atlético Madrid's stadium at almost every match since 1996. Blooming marvellous!

SPEEDO MICK

This tough Toffee is easy to spot at matches, since he is the only one wearing a pair of Everton swimming trunks! Mick got his nickname after swimming the Channel and now he attends all games in his tight blue Speedos, a swimming hat and goggles. What a splashing fan!

MEET THE SUPERFANS

When it comes to football lives, we can't forget the fans. These colourful characters are as keen as they come!

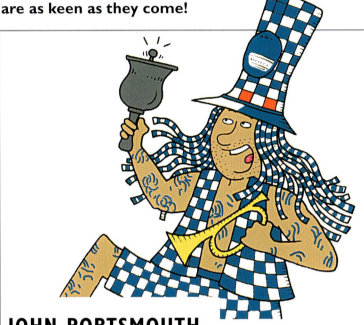

JOHN PORTSMOUTH FOOTBALL CLUB WESTWOOD

A bookseller by day, this superfan transforms himself during Pompey games. He wears a top hat and wig, and gets the crowd going by playing a bugle and ringing a handbell. John officially changed his middle names to the name of the club, and he has PFC engraved on his teeth. We love the way he sup-PORTS – and what a MOUTH!

CHRISTIAN KINNER

Borussia Dortmund fan Christian holds the world record for the longest football shout. He belted out *"Tor"* (German for "goal") for 43.56 seconds at a sound level above 80 decibels (about as loud as a lawnmower). *Tor*-iffic!

SILVIA GRECCO

When Brazilian mum Silvia takes her blind and autistic son Nickollas to watch his club Palmeiras, she narrates every moment of the game for him so as to make the experience as exciting as possible. For this she won the FIFA Fan Award in 2019.

MARGARITA LUENGO

Margarita has placed a bouquet of red and white carnations by the corner flag at Atlético Madrid's stadium at almost every match since 1996. Blooming marvellous!

SPEEDO MICK

This tough Toffee is easy to spot at matches, since he is the only one wearing a pair of Everton swimming trunks! Mick got his nickname after swimming the Channel and now he attends all games in his tight blue Speedos, a swimming hat and goggles. What a splashing fan!

TRAVEL MANAGER

Ever wondered how teams get to matches on time and always stay in nice hotels on away trips? That's down to me! I am a sensible planner, a good communicator and can make quick decisions when needed so I can provide the best travel options for large groups. It's an intense job, but rewarding when the players appreciate my work.

DATA SCIENTIST

I love using numbers and coding to find solutions. I collect, organize and interpret data to generate information that helps the club make decisions: this could be about a new player we want to sign, a tactical change because of an opposition weakness, or even season-ticket prices or how many shirts to stock in the club shop. I think almost any challenge can be overcome if you turn the question into a maths problem!

CLUB PHOTOGRAPHER

I go to training every day and take photos of the players in action. I send them to our media team, who put them on social media for our fans to enjoy. On match days, I stay in the background but get to access all areas (including the dressing room) to take the best possible photos. When a goal goes in, sometimes I run towards the scorer to capture the perfect shot.

GRAPHIC DESIGNER

I come up with cool design ideas that the club uses across its publications, such as the match programme, advertising campaigns and posters. I am super-creative and always thinking of new ways to use player and club imagery in interesting and fun ways, as long as they promote the club and engage fans and sponsors.

HEAD OF PLAYING SURFACES

I ensure that the training pitches and the stadium pitch are in ideal shape for the players. My team and I cut the grass, water and mark the pitches, and create fertilizer programmes to keep the grass as smooth as possible – even during winter. We are sustainable and recycle the grass for composting. I love being outdoors – even in the rain!

-JOBS IN FOOTBALL-

There are hundreds of jobs in football that do not involve being a player, coach or referee. Top clubs need experts to assist them in all sorts of ways. Here are just some of those jobs.

STADIUM EVENTS MANAGER

A football stadium usually hosts a match once every two weeks, which leaves a lot of time for other things: such as a conference, a wedding or a concert. I organize everything – from planning, promoting, hiring extra staff, managing budgets and smoothly hosting the event. I'm a good problem solver, enjoy meeting new people and love an event.

PLAYER CARE OFFICER

I look after new players and help them settle in; maybe finding them a house to live in, or a school for their children. I can set them up with a bank account and organize language lessons. Nothing is too difficult for me, because a happy player is a better player!

HEAD OF EDUCATION

I'm like a head teacher but at a football club! I make sure that every academy player across the age groups is benefiting from our lessons so they can reach their full potential. I love teaching and watching young people develop knowledge on and off the pitch!

COMMERCIAL MANAGER

I bring income into the club through four main avenues: sponsorship, advertising, hospitality and business partnerships. I need to build good relationships and be a strong salesperson as I'm convincing businesses to spend money. Smaller clubs rely on local businesses, but at a big club, the partners can be the biggest companies in the world.

KIT MANAGER

I make sure the players and coaches have clean kit ready to wear for training and match days. I lay out all the kit in the training ground or at the stadium on match days. I also oversee the washing of dirty kit and make sure the balls are pumped up and the goal nets are in good order. I am organized, punctual, fun to be around – and an early riser.

SPORTS MASSAGE THERAPIST

My job is to help players before and after training and matches. I give them massages to relax their muscles and ease tension or pain. During training, I'll work with injured players and will always listen if the players want to share any worries with me. I love working with players to help them get their bodies performing at their best.

HAVING A WORD WITH THE REF

We spoke to Darren England, a Premier League referee who has also taken charge of international games.

When did you realize you wanted to be a referee, and what was it that you found appealing about the role?

I first realized I wanted to be a referee when I knew I was not going to make it as a professional footballer. It was kind of a back-up plan. I like the fact that every game is different and you are working under high pressure, making decisions in a matter of seconds.

What are the skills that you need to be a good referee?

You have to be a good leader of your own team of officials and also the players, managers and the fans. You have to be able to manage people. You have to be resilient, as lots of people question your ability! Communication is a key skill, not just with words but also with your body language, which is what most people see on TV and in the stadiums.

How much time do you spend training?

I train around 5-6 days per week, as we have to be as fit as the players to keep up with the game!

Did you have another job before becoming a professional referee, and if so what was it?

I was also a football coach when I started refereeing. I coached for my local and favourite team, Barnsley. I used to coach the young, talented footballers in the academy and also deliver projects in the local community using the power of football to make people's lives better.

What is the hardest part of the job?

Making sure you do not make a mistake that impacts the outcome of the match. This is the worst thing for us.

How do you cope with the pressure of refereeing in a big match?

I try to prepare the same way for every match, which is to stay calm and relaxed. During the match I remain very focused and just take each decision I need to make, one at a time! I do not worry about past decisions in the game as it is all about the next decision!

What's your favourite part of the job?

Knowing that you can contribute positively to each game! Being part of memorable matches and memorable goals is also a great feeling. We have the next best view to the players, remember!

The World Cup is always an opportunity for national superfans like these to shine.

RIDHA JLASSI

Tunisia superfan Ridha is a work of art! He covers his body with paint in Tunisian colours. No one is redder than Ridha!

CLÉMENT D'ANTIBES

The Frenchman has been to every World Cup since 1982 and became famous for taking a cockerel (a symbol of France) to games, until attending games with live animals got banned.

EL COLE

Colombia's number one fan always dazzles as a colourful condor, a symbol of the Andean nations.

MANOLO, EL DEL BOMBO

Bombo means "bass drum" in Spanish, and Manolo has been beating the rhythm for Spain since 1982.

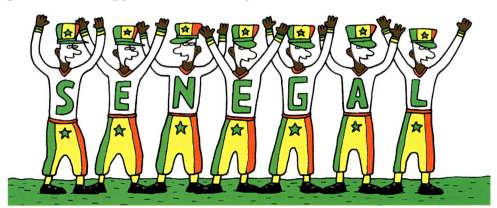

DOUZIÈME GAÏNDÉ

With a name that means "twelfth lion", this Senegalese fan group wear matching uniforms and dance choreographed moves. Pride of Africa!

-THE FOOTBALL FAMILY- QUIZ

1. **Around how much time, at the most, will a footballer spend playing football during their day at training?**

   a) One hour
   b) Ninety minutes
   c) Two hours
   d) Four hours

2. **What is the term for the tactical system in which a team soaks up pressure and then tries to score as soon as they win back the ball?**

   a) High press
   b) Diamond sprint
   c) Counter-attack
   d) Speedy-does-it

3. **In a 4–2–3–1 tactical system, what is the term given to the two midfielders?**

   a) Double pivot
   b) Double trouble
   c) Double threat
   d) Double dynamo

4. **Who is the most successful British coach of all time?**

   a) Brian Clough
   b) Vic Buckingham
   c) Valeriy Lobanovskyi
   d) Sir Alex Ferguson

5. **Most of the energy we get from food comes from carbohydrates. When do footballers eat the most carbohydrates?**

   a) Two days before a match
   b) One day before a match
   c) On the day of the match
   d) On the day after the match

6. **What do players have to do during a session of cryotherapy?**

   a) Sit for 3 minutes in temperatures of -150°C to restore their muscles
   b) Sit with a therapist and cry about their worries
   c) Swim in cold water to get fit
   d) Scream as loudly as possibly to release toxins from the body

7. **What is the youngest age group in which there are England teams?**

   a) Under-14 for men, Under-15 for women
   b) Under-15 for men, Under-16 for women
   c) Under-16 for men and women
   d) Under-17 for men and women

8. **John Portsmouth Football Club Westwood changed his middle names to include his favourite football team. How else did he show his support?**

   a) He engraved the letters "PFC" on his teeth.
   b) He named his child "Brick" after club founder John Brickwood.
   c) He had the name of every player from their 1950 title-winning season tattooed on his back.
   d) All of the above

9. **The volume of Borussia Dortmund fan Christian Kinner's shout of "Tooooor!" was over 80 decibels, which is about the same as which household item?**

   a) Loo flushing
   b) Chainsaw
   c) Lawnmower
   d) Fireworks

10. **Which of the following statements about a referee's kit is true?**

    a) The shirt must match the colour of the shorts and socks.
    b) The shirt, shorts and socks must be black.
    c) The shirt can be any colour as long as the shorts and socks are black.
    d) The shirt, shorts and socks must not match.

Answers: 1. b, 2. c, 3. a, 4. d, 5. b, 6. a, 7. b, 8. a, 9. c, 10. c.

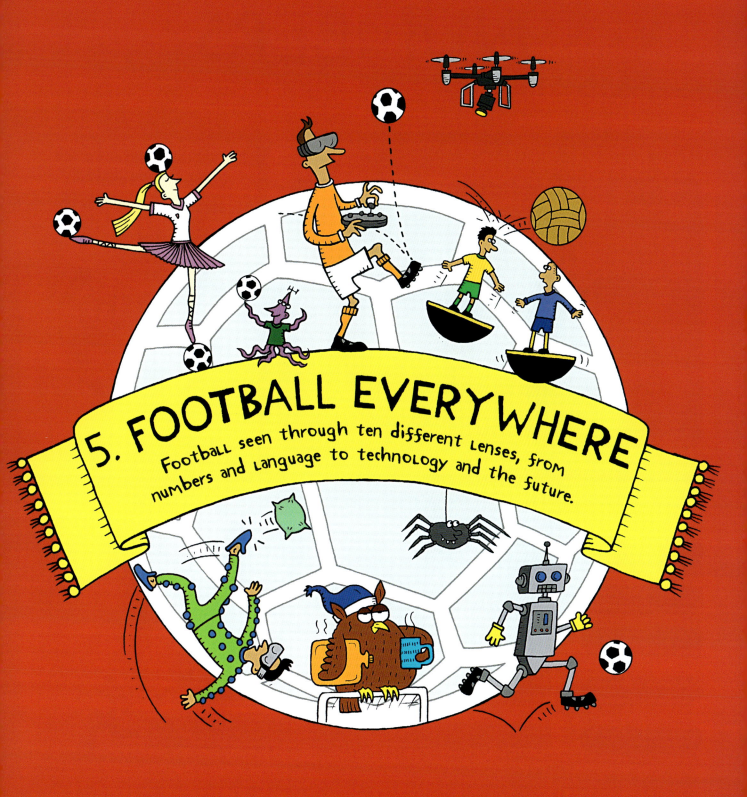

5. FOOTBALL EVERYWHERE

Football seen through ten different lenses, from numbers and language to technology and the future.

-FOOTBALL IN- NUMBERS

From scorelines to league tables, goal difference to distance covered, numbers are everywhere in football. Here are some of our favourite numerical nuggets.

Top five most common scores in English football:

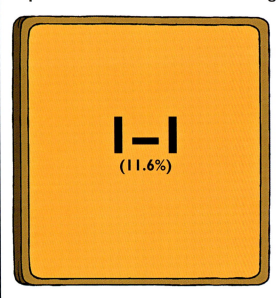

1–1
(11.6%)

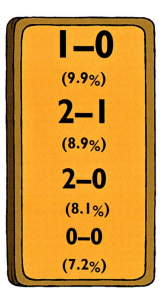

1–0
(9.9%)

2–1
(8.9%)

2–0
(8.1%)

0–0
(7.2%)

Numbers of balls used in a Premier League season:

3,800
(10 at every game)

Average distance run per game by position:

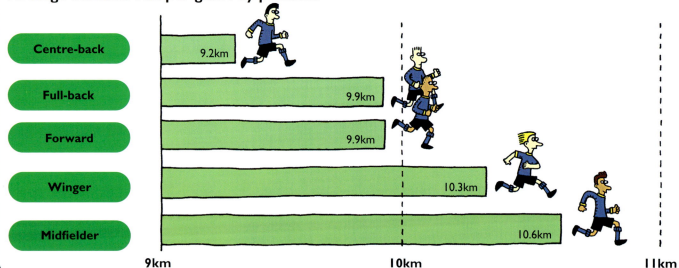

Position	Distance
Centre-back	9.2km
Full-back	9.9km
Forward	9.9km
Winger	10.3km
Midfielder	10.6km

9km   10km   11km

Average number of cards per game in different leagues:

 Best behaved league: Japan

 League closest to average: Luxembourg

 Naughtiest league: Bolivia

2.48 yellow cards
0.08 red cards

4.4 yellow cards
0.25 red cards

6.32 yellow cards
0.48 red cards

Chances of scoring a penalty if the shot is kicked in the following zones:

Average age in years per position across European leagues:

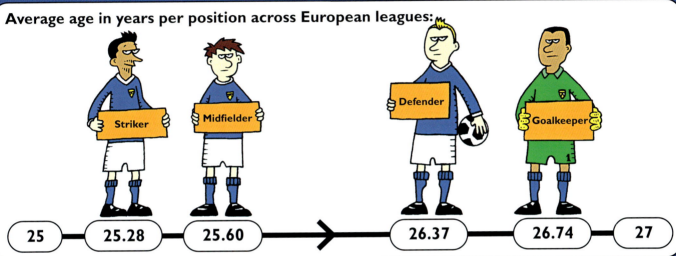

25	25.28	25.60		26.37	26.74	27
	Striker	Midfielder		Defender	Goalkeeper	

Average tenure of top-division coach across the world: **459** days
(1 year, 3 months and 2 days)

Average tenure of a Premier League coach: **772** days
(2 years, 1 month, 1 week and 4 days)

You're fired!

⊘ **Premier League Hall of Fame** ⊘

Most goals: Alan Shearer **260** goals

Most appearances: Gareth Barry **653** appearances

Played 1998–2006 for Southampton, Blackburn and Newcastle

Played 1998–2008 for Aston Villa, Manchester City, Everton and West Brom

Football Dictionary

The game we love is often described with words that are hard to understand. These football terms are ones that every fan needs to know.

advantage

The decision by the referee to play on after a foul, when the fouled team are in a better position than if the game was stopped.

aggregate

The combined score of two matches in a two-legged knockout tie. Each leg – one played at home, one away – represents a match.

bicycle kick

A kick struck with a player's back to the target, with the kicking leg raised as in the motion of riding a bike.

box-to-box player

A player who affects the game at both ends of the pitch, in a defensive and attacking way.

brace

When a player scores two goals in a match.

> I'm Brazil midfielder Ramires. I made history in 2011 when my two goals for Chelsea in a win over Stoke City made me the first Premier League player to score a brace while wearing a brace on my teeth. Smile!

clean sheet

When a goalkeeper or team does not concede a goal.

consolation goal

A goal scored by the losing team, usually late on, that does not affect the final result.

dead ball

The situation when the ball is started from a stationary position, such as a corner kick.

double

Either two victories, home and away, over a rival in the same league season; or when a team wins the league title and the cup competition in the same season.

fifty–fifty

Describes a challenge in which two players have an equal chance of winning the ball.

40 WAYS TO SCORE

There are many different ways to describe the act of scoring a goal. Here are 40 of them – can you think of any more?

belted, blasted, bundled, chipped, clipped, converted, crashed, curled, dinked, dipped, dispatched, drilled, drove, fired, flicked, floated, glanced, guided, hammered, hooked, lashed, nodded, passed, poked, powered, prodded, rammed, rifled, rolled, scrambled, slid, slotted, steered, stroked, swept, tapped, thumped, tipped, trickled, tucked

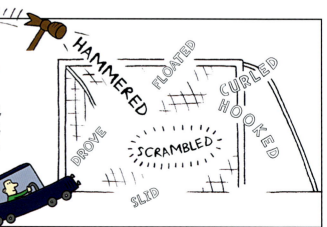

high press

A collective team effort to win the ball high up the pitch, near the opponent's goal. Also known by the German term *Gegenpressing*.

hospital ball

When an under-hit or misplaced pass puts a team-mate in danger of getting tackled or injured before gaining possession.

howler

A big mistake by a player, such as missing an open goal during a match.

limbs

Scenes of fans celebrating wildly, often jumping on top of each other, after a goal.

minnow

Named after a tiny fish, this refers to a small team that are not expected to win.

nutmeg

When a player plays the ball through an opponent's legs.

parking the bus

When the whole team plays defensively, as though there is a bus blocking the goal.

poacher

A player who regularly scores goals from close range.

route one

Direct style of football which involves long balls into the area.

scorpion kick

A move in which a player dives forward and kicks the ball with the soles of their feet. Made famous by Colombian goalkeeper René Higuita.

screamer

An amazing goal, usually scored from long distance.

sitter

An easy chance to score. Can be either scored or missed.

stalwart

A player who has stayed at one club for a long time.

top flight

The highest league in each country's football pyramid.

worldy

A goal considered world-class.

BINS, OWLS AND SCISSORS

Every player loves to score a goal by firing the ball into the top corner of the net. In England, that area of the goal is known as "top bins" – although no one knows exactly why. In other countries, that area of the goal is described in different ways: in Algeria, it's called "where the devil sleeps"; in Brazil, "where the owl sleeps"; in Egypt, "in the scissors"; in France, "the attic window"; in Italy, "the seven"; in the Netherlands, "the carpenter's ruler"; in Russia, "the nine"; in Spain, "where the spiders nest"; and in the USA, "the upper 90". What a top bin-anza!

-FOOTBALL-
AND THE MEDIA

Newspapers, radio, TV and the Internet have all shaped how we watch and think about football.

THE F⚽⚽TBALL TIMES

Newspapers champion exciting new sport

Football became the game we know today thanks to the media, meaning the vehicles of mass communication such as newspapers, magazines, radio, TV, apps and websites. In fact, football and the media have helped each other flourish since Victorian times.

The story began with newspapers, which had a huge impact on football in the late nineteenth century. Match reports and fixture lists helped sell papers, and the papers, in turn, promoted football, gaining it new fans and turning the sport into a subject of national interest. At the beginning of the twentieth century, almost all of the UK's regional daily papers (and there were well over one hundred of them) started Saturday sports newspapers that appeared around an hour after the final whistle in Saturday's games. These papers – often on pink or green paper – had a match report of the game by the local team, and all the national results and tables. Fans would pick them up on the way home. The last remaining Saturday sports paper, Portsmouth's *Sports Mail*, closed in 2022, after 119 years.

Newspapers also began to write about the personal lives of players, turning them into celebrities, and introduced pundits giving opinion and analysis. You can't imagine a newspaper now without its sports pages!

Contribution: Newspapers raised the profile of football in its early days, making it a topic of national discussion.

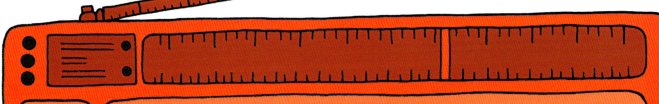

Radio turns up the game

The second means of communication to change football was an invention called the wireless – or radio – that entered people's homes in the 1920s. In January 1927, the newly-formed British Broadcasting Corporation (BBC) broadcast its first live match on the radio, between Arsenal and Sheffield United. Worried that listeners would find it hard to visualize what was going on, the station asked the *Radio Times* (the BBC's magazine) to print a plan of the pitch divided into eight numbered areas. The commentator referred to the numbers of the areas during his commentary, in order for the listeners to understand where the ball was!

In the following decades, radio became one of the most important ways that fans followed football. Fans listened to big matches in real time from their home or while driving in the car, and also got results from around the country as soon as they happened. Radio also created an important new role within the game: the commentator. British commentators are generally dispassionate when they talk about the game, but commentators in other countries are sometimes more concerned about creating excitement. That's how one Brazilian radio presenter came up with the cry "gooooooool". What a guuuuuuuuuy!

Contribution: Radio gave fans at home the collective experience of listening to live football.

Football is the greatest show on Earth

Football has made its mark on TV and vice versa. For a start, the most watched TV broadcast in UK history was the 1966 World Cup final between England and West Germany, with 32.3 million viewers, more than half the population of the country. Not bad considering only 75 per cent of homes had a TV at the time and they were all black-and-white! Colour TV was introduced in 1969, and the 1970 World Cup was the first tournament to be broadcast in colour.

Today, football draws such large TV audiences that TV companies pay organizations like the Premier League, the FA and FIFA billions of pounds to secure the rights to broadcast games. (The companies then recoup this money through subscriptions and selling advertising slots.) The huge sums involved have changed the game: by increasing the salaries of players so that the top ones earn millions every year and also by organizing the fixture list so that as many games as possible can be shown live.

Contribution: TV has made football the richest sport in the world and brought it to an audience of billions.

On the Internet, football is available all day long

The online world has completely changed the experience of being a fan. Whatever you want to find out about your club, you can now do so at any time and from anywhere in the world at the touch of a button. Clubs' websites offer exclusive news, interviews and videos, and football players and teams are among the most searched terms in Wikipedia. Fans have more facts available to them than ever before – it's a football fact-ory!

Social media has also become an important forum for fans to discuss the game, share stories and make friends. The visibility of fan groups online has meant that fans' voices have never been heard so loudly. It has also brought players closer to fans, since many players have social media profiles from which they often share their opinions or details of their lives. Many of the people with the biggest number of followers on social media are footballers. In fact, one of the people with the most followers on Instagram and Facebook is Cristiano Ronaldo.

Contribution: The Internet has brought players and clubs closer to their fans – who have facts and figures at their fingertips.

-FOOTBALL'S-
BIGGEST DEBATES

Football is a game of opinions. No, it's not! Yes, it is! We love it because everyone can have a different point of view – and we can still get on! Here, we argue over some of football's biggest unresolved questions.

GREATEST MALE PLAYER OF ALL TIME

PELÉ   V.   LIONEL MESSI

REASONS FOR:

★ Only player in history to win three World Cups
★ Scored over 1,000 goals
★ Made Brazil famous worldwide

REASONS FOR:

★ Won a record seven Ballon d'Or titles
★ Averaged almost one goal per game over fifteen seasons
★ World's best passer, dribbler and finisher

REASONS AGAINST:

★ Never played in a top European league
★ Slower defenders, so easier to score goals then
★ Supported by other world-class Brazil players

REASONS AGAINST:

★ Only won one World Cup with Argentina
★ Easy to win with Barcelona as they were a great team
★ Average record from the penalty spot

VERDICT:

PELÉ! Goals mean more than Ballons d'Or!

MESSI! Football is harder to play now!

GREATEST FEMALE PLAYER OF ALL TIME

MARTA   V.   MIA HAMM

REASONS FOR:

★ Won six World Player of the Year titles
★ Women's World Cup all-time top scorer
★ Inspired current Brazilian generation

REASONS FOR:

★ Won two World Cups and two Olympic golds
★ Scored a then-record 158 international goals
★ First female footballer endorsed by brands

REASONS AGAINST:

★ Missed a penalty in 2007 World Cup final
★ Never won the World Cup
★ Lost three out of four European Cup finals

REASONS AGAINST:

★ Was surrounded by superb team-mates
★ Team tactics were set up for her to score
★ Reluctant hero: didn't enjoy the spotlight

VERDICT:

MARTA! Brazil's best of the best!

MIA! Changed women's football for ever!

BEST GOAL EVER SCORED

DIEGO MARADONA
ARGENTINA GOAL V. ENGLAND IN
1986 WORLD CUP QUARTER-FINAL

V.

CARLI LLOYD
USA GOAL V. JAPAN IN 2015
WORLD CUP FINAL

REASONS FOR:

★ Solo dribble which started inside his own half
★ Dribbled past six opponents then goalkeeper
★ Voted FIFA's Goal of the Century

REASONS AGAINST:

★ Earlier in game he scored a handball
★ England's defence was poor
★ It was selfish of him not to pass

REASONS FOR:

★ Jinked the ball past opponent to make the chance
★ Lobbed the goalkeeper from the halfway line
★ The goal was her third in a 16-minute spell

REASONS AGAINST:

★ Game was already over by then
★ Goalkeeper was too far off her line
★ Kicking the ball a long way isn't that skilled

VERDICT:

DIEGO! Maradona gonna winna!

CARLI! Let's laud Lloyd's long lob!

BEST KIT EVER WORN

PERU 1978

V.

ENGLAND 1966

REASONS FOR:

★ Diagonal sash is dramatic, rare, and stands out
★ Clean and visually pleasing design
★ Voted the best World Cup shirt of all time

REASONS AGAINST:

★ Team wasn't very successful
★ Not very colourful
★ Diagonals are rare for a reason

REASONS FOR:

★ Most iconic football shirt ever
★ England won 1966 World Cup wearing it
★ Teams in all-red win more matches

REASONS AGAINST:

★ One colour is a bit boring
★ A round neck collar is old-fashioned
★ Short sleeves are more practical

VERDICT:

PERUUUU! Stylish, cool and unique – like me!

ENGLAND! Classic, elegant and old – like me!

-FOOTBALL-
TRAGEDIES

Many disasters have befallen the football world, causing the horrific deaths of players and fans. It's important to remember those who died and to do everything we can to prevent similar events ever happening again.

PLANE CRASHES

Several teams have been involved in plane crashes. Thankfully, flying is much safer now than it used to be.

1949: Torino, who at that time were the best team in Italy and the backbone of the national side, were returning from a friendly when their plane crashed in dense fog, hitting the wall of a church on a hill in Turin. The team, including their English coach, all died.

1958: English champions Manchester United were flying back from a European Cup tie in Yugoslavia when they stopped in Munich to refuel. Slush on the runway caused the plane to crash during take-off, an accident that killed 23 of the 44 people on board, including eight players, many of whom played for England. The crash created huge sympathy for United, and is one of the reasons why they became the best supported club in England.

1993: Eighteen members of the Zambia national team died in a plane crash on their way to a World Cup qualifier. Remarkably, Zambia reached the final of the 1994 Africa Cup of Nations, even though the nation was still in mourning and their newly assembled team had barely had any time to train together. They were 1–0 up against Nigeria after three minutes, but ended up losing 2–1 to take the runners-up medals.

2016: Brazilian side Chapecoense reached the final of the Copa Sudamericana, the South American version of the Europa League. En route to the second leg of the final in Colombia, the plane carrying the squad, staff and journalists ran out of fuel and crashed, killing 71 of the 77 people on board. The final was never played, and the club was awarded the title.

Chapecoense players, including three survivors of the crash, with the Sudamericana trophy

STADIUM DISASTERS

British stadiums are now very safe to visit. One reason is that many lessons have been learned from previous disasters, such as these four.

COLLAPSE

Ibrox Park, Glasgow, 1902

Glasgow Rangers' new stadium hosted a Scotland–England match with 68,000 in attendance, which was the first time the stadium was almost full to capacity. One of the wooden stands collapsed, causing around 250 people to fall to the concrete floor below, of whom 25 died.

Aftermath: Architects stopped using wood and steel for stands, choosing reinforced concrete instead.

FIRE

Valley Parade, Bradford, 1985

At a Bradford City home game, a cigarette stub fell between the floorboards of the stand and a pile of rubbish below caught fire. The blaze engulfed the stand: 56 fans died, either suffocated by smoke, crushed or burned.

Aftermath: The disaster led to new safety standards being introduced at UK grounds. Bradford wear a black trim on their shirts in memory of those who died.

HOOLIGANISM

Heysel Stadium, Belgium, 1985

Shortly before the European Cup final between Liverpool and Juventus, a few Liverpool fans began to attack Juventus fans. A stadium wall collapsed and 39 people were killed, almost all of them Italians.

Aftermath: Fourteen Liverpool fans were convicted of manslaughter. English clubs were banned from European competitions for five years, Liverpool for six years. New rules were introduced to fight hooliganism.

CRUSH

Hillsborough, Sheffield, 1989

An FA Cup semi-final between Liverpool and Nottingham Forest, at Sheffield Wednesday's stadium, ended in tragedy when police trying to ease congestion outside the stadium opened a gate to let Liverpool fans in. The fans walked into the stands without knowing they were already overcrowded and many fans were crushed against the pitch-side fencing. In total, 97 fans died.

Aftermath: An investigation concluded police error was to blame. The disaster led to many changes, such as clubs removing the fencing between the stands and the pitch, and converting stadiums to all-seater stands.

The Hillsborough Memorial at Anfield, Liverpool's stadium, has the names of all the victims, and a flame that never goes out.

-UNFAIR PLAY-

Some players are notorious for bad behaviour.
Let's gawp at the ugly side of the beautiful game.

LUIS SUÁREZ

Uruguay's all-time top scorer was famously goal-hungry – he had a reputation for biting his opponents. He bit players in the Dutch Eredivisie, the Premier League and at the 2014 World Cup, receiving multiple-match bans every time. Those punishments were certainly something to chew on!

GERARDO BEDOYA

The Colombian defensive midfielder has received more red cards than any other player in history: 46. No other player has more than 30! He retired in 2015 and went into coaching. And guess what: after 21 minutes of his coaching debut he was sent off for arguing with the referee!

VINNIE JONES

The unsmiling defender got a reputation as a hard man playing for Premier League clubs including Chelsea and Wimbledon in the 1990s. He was fined by the FA for appearing on a video that gave tips on how to scare opponents. When he retired, he became a film actor who played criminals and villains.

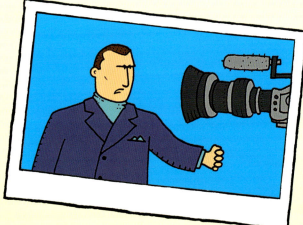

ZINEDINE ZIDANE

The former France midfielder (and now coach) is one of the best players of all-time. He led France to the 2006 World Cup final and received the Golden Ball as player of the tournament. Yet that final also saw his most notorious performance – he headbutted his Italy opponent in the chest and was sent off – a shocking finale to a great career.

MATCH-FIXING

Match-fixing is when players or officials act dishonestly in trying to influence the result of a game. It is usually done for financial gain: the fixers hope to make lots of money by ensuring results go a certain way.

CASE 1: THE CALCIOPOLI SCANDAL

This was the greatest scandal in Italian football history, in which top clubs, including Juventus, Milan and Lazio, were discovered to have been putting pressure on the league to choose referees more favourable to them. As a result, Juventus were relegated from Serie A in 2006, for the first time in their history, and the other clubs received points deductions.

CASE 2: SUSPICIOUS SCORELINES

Level on points in a Sierra Leone league in 2022, Gulf and Kahunla Rangers knew that the team with the best goal difference would get promoted. On the last day of the season, their respective matches ended 91–1 and 95–0! The Sierra Leone FA ordered an immediate investigation into whether the losing teams deliberately lost. Surely not!

JAILBIRDS

These two players went from football glory to prison infamy.

PÅL ENGER

One of Norway's most notorious thieves started off as a promising teenage footballer at Oslo side Vålerenga, playing for them in the UEFA Cup (the precursor of the Europa League). His biggest heist came in 1994, when he snuck into an art gallery in Oslo and stole Edvard Munch's *The Scream*, one of the world's most famous paintings – a crime for which he was sentenced to six and a half years in prison.

RONALDINHO

The Brazilian two-time FIFA Player of the Year spent his 40th birthday in a maximum-security prison in Paraguay after police discovered he and his brother arrived in the country using fake passports. When in jail, he played futsal with inmates and his team won the prison tournament. After a month in prison, he spent four more months detained in a hotel, before he was freed.

-FOOTBALL-
TECHNOLOGY

In the quest for better results and improved performances, players, clubs and referees have turned to technology. Here are some high-tech tools that are changing how we play, watch and even officiate the game.

① WEARABLE TRACKER

What is it? Sensors on boots

Who is it used by? Players

How does it work? Smart sensors are strapped onto the boot and measure every micromovement, including impact with the ground, the ball and rotation of each foot. The sensors sync to an app, allowing players to track their performance, breaking it down into work rate (distance covered and sprints), technique (ball touches by foot and kicking speed) and tempo (one touches, short possessions, top speed).

What's the benefit? The data allows amateur and professional players, and their coaches, to track their performance over time, monitoring aspects of their technical and physical game to see where improvements can be made.

TRACKER

② INJURY PREDICTOR

What is it? An app that detects players at risk of injury

Who is it used by? Coaches and doctors

How does it work? Player information, such as game and training data, strength, sleep, flexibility and stress levels are uploaded to the app. The app uses an algorithm to calculate a daily forecast showing the player's likelihood to sustain an injury over the next seven days. If a certain player is at risk of injury, then their training programme can be changed.

What's the benefit? Injured players can't help the team. Every coach wants as many healthy players as possible to select from – more available players might mean more wins!

③ DRONE

What is it? An aircraft with a camera to film training from above

Who is it used by? Coaches and players

How does it work? A licensed drone pilot films training sessions and downloads the bird's-eye footage to coaches, who make clips to illustrate points around positioning and space for players.

What's the benefit? Players can see exactly where they are on the pitch in certain situations and can adjust accordingly. The aerial footage makes it easier for them to learn and improve.

④ VIRTUAL REALITY SIMULATED FOOTBALL GAME

What is it? A tool to improve decision-making

Who is it used by? Players, especially ones who are injured

How does it work? Players wear a headset that transports them into a football match. They receive the virtual ball and make passes by kicking out their feet. Their eye movements and awareness of what's around them are measured, as is the speed and quality of their decision-making. The players can use this data to improve their game.

What's the benefit? Regular users, such as Norway's Martin Ødegaard, say that the immersive tool helps teach them to make the right pass at the right time. It can also be used by injured players as no physical training is required.

⑤ VIDEO ASSISTANT REFEREE (VAR)

What is it? Replay system to help referees avoid mistakes

Who is it used by? Referees

How does it work? During a game, a qualified referee watches slow-motion replays on TV screens to alert the on-pitch referee in case of a clear mistake or missed incident relating to a goal, a penalty, a direct red card or mistaken identity. The VAR only advises; the referee always has the final decision.

What's the benefit? Technology is there to help reduce important mistakes because the game is so fast that officials can't always make the right decisions without help from replays. And even then, they still occasionally get it wrong!

In the Premier League, VARs are not based at the stadium. They watch matches from a TV studio in Stockley Park, which is near Heathrow Airport in West London. They are joined by an Assistant VAR (who makes sure nothing is missed while the VAR is replaying an incident) and an RO (Replay Operator).

-FOOTBALL-
EVERYWHERE

The game has inspired many, many variations. Here we choose our favourites from around the world.

FUTSAL

History: Founded in Uruguay in the 1930s as a way to play football indoors, futsal quickly spread through South America because it meant football could be played whatever the weather. There are now professional leagues in countries including Brazil, Spain, Russia and Portugal. Since 1989, FIFA has organized the four-yearly Futsal World Cup.

Rules: Five-a-side. Indoors on a hard floor. Two twenty-minute halves, with time stopping every dead ball. Each team can have a one-minute time-out per half. Unlimited substitutions from a squad of twelve. No offsides. Ball is smaller and less bouncy than a standard football.

Most successful nation: Brazil

Star: Max Kilman played 25 times for the England national futsal team and then signed for Wolves in the Premier League.

BEACH FOOTBALL

History: Began in Rio de Janeiro, Brazil, where football fans have long played on the beach. Beach football spread beyond Brazil in the 1990s and FIFA became the governing body in 2005. The Beach Soccer World Cup takes place every two years.

Rules: Five-a-side. Sand pitch. Three periods of twelve minutes. No draws. Three minutes of extra time, and a penalty shoot-out if needed. Unlimited substitutions from a squad of twelve. No offsides. No shoes!

Most successful nation: Brazil

Star: Switzerland's Noël Ott is known as the Lionel Messi of beach football.

FREESTYLE FOOTBALL

History: Freestyling is the art of doing tricks with a football. It used to be considered a circus routine until players like Diego Maradona in the 1980s began to delight fans by showing off ball-juggling skills during pre-match warm-ups. The sport took off in the Internet age, as players developed new moves and shared videos online. The World Freestyle Football Association was founded in 2017, and it estimates about 15,000 athletes compete in its competitions, of whom a few hundred are professionals.

Rules: Competitive freestyling is often performed as a battle between two contestants. In the most prestigious event, Red Bull Street Style, two contestants battle over three minutes. They take turns to juggle the ball for a maximum of 30 seconds each. Judges select the winners based on difficulty, originality, execution, performance, surprise and all-round ability. No hands on the ball at any stage!

Star: Londoner Lia Lewis trained as a ballet dancer, saw a freestyling video on Instagram and three years later became world champion.

 SWAMP FOOTBALL

Originating in Finland and popular in Scotland, swamp football is played on mud.

ROBOT FOOTBALL

The RoboCup has run every year since 1997 so computer scientists can try out their latest football-playing robots.

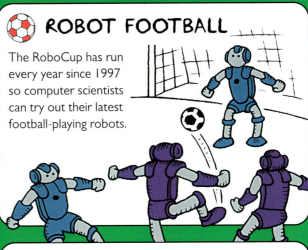

TABLE FOOTBALL

Also known as foosball, table football is played by swivelling model footballers fixed to metal rods. No spinning allowed!

SUBBUTEO

A tabletop game invented in 1946, it is played with tiny model footballers on weighted round bases.

-FOOTBALL FOR ALL-

Many football variations exist for people with disabilities. They ensure the game is accessible to as many people as possible. Each of the sports below has a national league and international games.

POWERCHAIR FOOTBALL

A fast-moving game played by electric wheelchair users on an indoor pitch, with four on each side.

AMPUTEE FOOTBALL

A seven-a-side game for amputees and people with restricted use of limbs. Players use crutches for balance.

DEAF FOOTBALL

The game has the same rules as football, but the ref uses a flag rather than a whistle.

CEREBRAL PALSY FOOTBALL

Played seven-a-side and outdoors, with two halves of 30 minutes.

BLIND FOOTBALL

A five-a-side game with four blind outfield players and a sighted or partially sighted keeper. Players use their ears to locate the ball, which contains metal shards that make a noise when it rolls. Spectators are quiet at all times.

-FOOTBALL-
COMPUTER GAMES

People spend more time playing football on computers than playing in real life. In some computer games, you're the head coach and in others, you are the player. Here are some of football's most popular games.

FIFA

In this video game, originally produced in association with the game's governing body FIFA, you take on the role of the players, using a console to control their movements and decisions on the pitch. Depending on whether your team has the ball or not, you can decide if your player should make a short pass, long pass, through-ball or shot. There are other game modes, including Career Mode, where you take control of a single person, either a player or coach, and manage their career through the choices you make.

The game is the most popular football computer game in history and opened up football to millions of new fans. *FIFA* allows newcomers to the sport to learn about players, teams and their skills – and to experience playing as them in 3D on-pitch simulations of matches. A new release every year builds anticipation around the cover stars (*FIFA 23* had Kylian Mbappé and Sam Kerr), while the game awards each player a single rating figure (out of 100) based on their attributes – which they often complain about!

In 2022, FIFA (the governing body) decided it would make the game without the help of EA Sports, the company that originally created the game in 1995. The existing version, beloved by so many, will continue under the name of *EA Sports FC*.

FIFA HIGHEST-RANKED PLAYERS OF ALL TIME

FIFA gives players ratings out of 100. Here are the highest ratings they have ever given to players:

PLAYER	COUNTRY	YEAR	CLUB	RATING
Ronaldo	Brazil			
Ronaldo	Brazil	2004	Real Madrid	98
Luís Figo	Portugal	2000	Inter-nazionale	97
Matteo Brighi	Italy	2002	Barcelona	97
Thierry Henry	France	2003	Juventus	97
Gigi Buffon	Italy	2005	Arsenal	97
		2005	Juventus	97

325 Million
Total number of copies of FIFA sold worldwide since it launched in 1995. The FIFA series is the best-selling video game in the world. The combined total of FIFA 23 matches played is already over 7.5 billion.

FIFAe WORLD CUP

E-sports is competitive video game-playing. One of the biggest e-sports tournaments in the world is the FIFAe World Cup. Qualification is like the real World Cup – except for the number of players! Millions of FIFA players enter in regional competitions for the chance to reach the final 32, when the competition is narrowed down into group stages and then a knockout tournament. In 2022, Umut Gületkin, a nineteen-year-old German, was crowned world champion. As well as the coveted trophy, he won £200,000!

FOOTBALL MANAGER

Football Manager is the video game in which you take on the role of Team Manager by signing players, managing budgets and selecting tactics. You can pick any team to coach and start at any level in the football pyramid. Each player has around 200 individual attributes (marked out of 20) that define how they will play: all those numbers feed into an algorithm which creates a decision that each player will make once the game kicks off. Every match contains almost half a million decisions! The amount of detail, all based on real data, is so great that professional teams often use the game to help with their scouting.

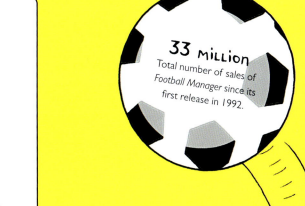

33 million
Total number of sales of *Football Manager* since its first release in 1992.

CARPE DÍAZ

A football scout, working for the Chile national team, spotted on *Football Manager* that a striker at English club Blackburn Rovers had a mother born in Chile. That's how Ben Brereton, now known as Ben Brereton Díaz, became a striker and, after scoring some important goals, a national hero in Chile.

FANTASY PREMIER LEAGUE

Fantasy Premier League is played on a computer or smartphone. You select a squad of fifteen players (two goalkeepers, five defenders, five midfielders, three forwards) currently in the Premier League, within an imaginary budget of £100 million. Each player is given a value, the total of which has to fit your budget. Your team then gets points based on the players' real-life performances, according to goals, assists, saves and clean sheets. Double points are available every week for the captain, and bonus points if a player is the top performer in the match. Run by the Premier League, everyone competes in one giant league (featuring millions of players) but you can set up your own mini-league so you can compete with your friends and family.

9 million
Total number of players subscribed to the FPL 2022–23 season. This makes it the biggest fantasy league game in the world.

CHECKMATE!

World chess champion Magnus Carlsen loves playing *FPL* – and he's really good at it! The Norwegian finished eleventh out of over seven million players in 2021, and always watches games and analyses statistics to give himself the best chance of success. "In terms of what gives me the most happiness, I would say winning *FPL* would trump everything except becoming World Champion in classical chess," he once said.

-THE FUTURE OF-
FOOTBALL

It's the end of the book, but not the end of football! Here we give our predictions of where the game might go.

2030

FANS IN CHARGE

Increasingly, fans will get more of a say in club decisions. Already some clubs ask their supporters to help choose a new club badge or team kit. But in the future, clubs may run polls during matches to help decide what substitutions the coach should make, who the next manager should be or what players they should buy.

2035

EUROPEAN SUPER LEAGUE

Europe's biggest clubs tried in 2021 to set up an exclusive league just for them, so they didn't need to compete in their national leagues. Plans were dropped after a public backlash: fans argued it was greedy, and went against the all-inclusive spirit of football. It is inevitable the clubs will try again – and maybe next time they will succeed.

2040

RULE CHANGES

Advances in training, nutrition and tactics will make football even faster and more physical. Players' bodies will be pushed to their limits – which means there will be an increased risk of injuries and burnout. FIFA may be forced to introduce new rules such as allowing more substitutes, shortening the length of the game or introducing time-outs.

2045

DATA DELUGE

More and more data will be available to clubs and fans, perhaps including measurements of neuronal activity in footballers' brains, maps of where their eyes are looking, and instantaneous read-outs of kick-strength. Maybe fans will have trackers too so you know how loud they are screaming and how nervous they are at crucial moments.

2050

CLIMATE

The world is heating up, causing glaciers to melt and the sea-level to rise. Based on current trends, some experts say that Hull City and Cardiff City's grounds will be entirely underwater by 2050 and a quarter of all English stadiums will be at risk of flooding. In order to reduce carbon emissions, players and fans may no longer fly to away matches.

2060

METAVERSE

The metaverse is a virtual 3D world that you can explore wearing a virtual reality headset and a haptic suit. As the technology improves, it will become possible to play football in the metaverse against avatars of your favourite players. It will mean you can get the sensation of playing in front of a full Wembley crowd from your own bedroom!

2070

| CHINA | 6 |
| BRAZIL | 0 |

BALANCE OF POWER

Football's strongest continents are currently Europe and South America. But this could easily change. The potential for growth in China, for example, which has a population of about 1.5 billion people and where football is growing fast, is huge! It is very possible that one day the China men's national team will win the World Cup.

2080

ROBOTS

One day robots will play football better than humans: they will be stronger, never tire and always make perfect decisions. Clubs may develop teams of robot footballers for a robot football league. In this way, football may become more like Formula 1, where rules about what technology is accepted are updated every season.

2090

Tackling   Passing   Shooting

CYBORGS

Humans in 2100 may be very different from how they are now. People may be able to edit their genes so they can become taller, stronger or better at football. Injuries may become a thing of the past as humans are able to replace damaged body parts with artificial limbs that have been specially designed for football tasks.

2100

SPACE

If we set up a colony on the Moon or Mars, the residents of these distant places will want to play football. Since gravity is weaker on both the Moon and Mars, players will be able to jump much higher than on Earth, and the ball will bounce higher and travel further. The rules of football in space will need to be changed to take this into account.

-FOOTBALL EVERYWHERE-
QUIZ

1. **What colour shirts did England wear when they won the 1966 World Cup final?**

   a) Red
   b) White
   c) Blue
   d) Red, white and blue

2. **Where was beach football founded?**

   a) Bondi, Australia
   b) Rio de Janeiro, Brazil
   c) Blackpool, England
   d) Miami, USA

3. **Which type of football was founded in Finland?**

   a) Futsal
   b) Powerchair football
   c) Table football
   d) Swamp football

4. **What is Colombian midfielder Gerardo Bedoya's footballing claim to fame?**

   a) He was banned from football for farting at the referee.
   b) He was sent off 46 times, more than anyone else in history.
   c) He captained his country and went on to become a movie star.
   d) He was arrested by Scotland Yard after he stole a sack of turf from Wembley during a friendly against England.

5. **Norwegian footballer Pål Enger was jailed for which crime?**

   a) He stole a famous painting, *The Scream*, from a gallery in Oslo.
   b) He used a fake passport to go on holiday to Paraguay.
   c) He was arrested after he bit three opponents.
   d) He deliberately missed an open goal during the Norwegian cup final and was sued by a fan group.

6. **The first football match to be broadcast on radio in 1927 was between which teams?**

   a) Liverpool v. Everton
   b) Manchester United v. Preston North End
   c) Arsenal v. Sheffield United
   d) Rangers v. Celtic

7. **Which football match drew the biggest-ever UK TV audience of over 32 million people?**

   a) England v. West Germany in 1966
   b) Manchester United v. Barcelona in 1999
   c) England v. Italy in 2021
   d) England Women v. Germany Women in 2022

8. **What is the most common score in football?**

   a) 0–1
   b) 1–0
   c) 1–1
   d) 2–1

9. **In which country's league are players shown the most red and yellow cards per game?**

   a) Japan
   b) Russia
   c) Luxembourg
   d) Bolivia

10. **What is the term used to describe scenes of fans celebrating wildly, often jumping on top of each other?**

    a) Limbs
    b) Jumps
    c) Scenes
    d) FanFun

Answers: 1.a, 2.b, 3.d, 4.b, 5.a, 6.c, 7.a, 8.c, 9.d, 10.a

-INDEX-

-ACKNOWLEGEMENTS-

Here's one final fact for you: Spike Gerrell is the world's greatest football illustrator! Spike is a Football School stalwart whose drawings contain screamers and worldies in equal measure. Thank you, Spike. Your sketching sorcery is top bins – no debate!

We also know how important the team behind the team is. The structure of our team is similar to a football club: head of football operations is our brilliant editor Daisy Jellicoe, with Denise Johnstone-Burt, Louise Jackson, Laurélie Bazin, Faith Leung, Charlie Wilson and Rebecca Oram providing invaluable help along the way. Thanks also to our agent Rebecca Carter and the backroom staff at Janklow & Nesbit and David Luxton Associates.

We were constantly learning about football as we wrote this book, and are grateful to our friends who shared their knowledge with us too: Ed Aarons, Ben Campbell at PGMOL, Stuart Carrington, Darren England, Jamie Fahey, Justin Goodchild, Nick Harris, Jordi Mestre at the World Freestyle Football Association, Maher Mezahi, Matt Mills at Beach Soccer Worldwide, Kevin Nicholson, Thorsten Sterzing, Craig Umenyi, Andy Walker at the FA, Eleanor Watson, Dave Wetherall at the EFL, Saskia Whitfield, and the Wigan Athletic crew, Ash Houghton, Jay Whittle and Diane Winnard. Thank you!

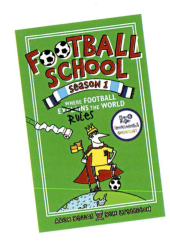

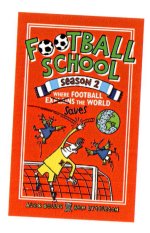

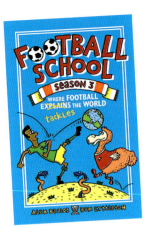

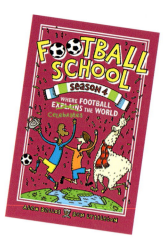

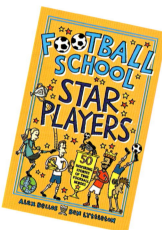

COLLECT THE
FOOTBALL SCHOOL SERIES

footballschool.co
youtube.com/FootballSchoolFacts

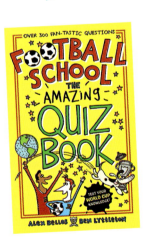

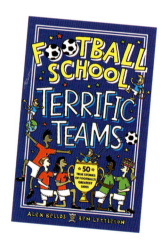

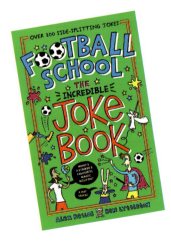

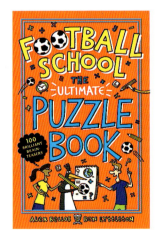

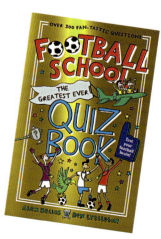